Welcome to Multilingual Joomla Explained.

Our names are Igor Mihaljko and Steve Burge.

Igor speaks English and Croatian. He also understands German (if you speak really slowly).

Steve speaks British English, American English and is pretty good with Spanish, and Japanese.

In this book, we'll show you how to build multilingual websites using Joomla.

This book starts with an introduction to multilingual sites and the different approaches you can take to create a multilingual site.

After the first two chapters, this becomes a practical, hands-on book. Follow on with the exercises in this book, and you'll learn how to build a website in two languages. For the purpose of this book, we'll show you how to build a multilingual Joomla site in English and French.

The knowledge you learn will help you create websites in other languages, and in more than two languages.

The content of this book is meant for all Joomla users, from novice users to those who have been using Joomla for years.

THIS BOOK IS ACTIVE

You don't learn to ride a bicycle by reading a book: You learn by actually riding.

You don't learn to drive a car by reading a book: You learn by actually driving.

A book can help and give some advice, but without actually riding a bike or driving a car, you'll never really learn. The same is true with Joomla.

So, throughout every chapter of this book, you're going to be asked to work with Joomla.

THIS BOOK USES ALMOST NO CODE

You do not need to know any HTML and CSS to use this book. That is a deliberate decision because we want to make this book accessible to ordinary people. We believe you don't have to be a developer to use Joomla.

However, that will disappoint some of you because this book does talk about adding multilingual features to your own code. If you do know CSS and PHP and want to dive into more advanced topics, there's a lot of advanced training at https://ostraining.com/classes/joomla.

THINGS IN THIS BOOK WILL CHANGE

Joomla changes regularly, and so do the extra features and designs that you add on to it.

Everything in this book is correct at the time of writing. However, it's possible that some of the instructions and screen shots may become out-of-date.

Be patient with any changes you find. Email us at books@ostraining.com if you think any has changed. People do that all the time, and we include a big "Thank You!" to them in the next update of the book.

WHAT YOU NEED FOR THIS BOOK

Now that you know a little bit about this book, let's make sure you're ready to follow along.

You need only two things to follow along with the exercises in this book:

- A computer with an Internet connection
- A hosting account or computer where you can install Joomla

Yes, that 's really all you need.

ABOUT JOOMLASHACK

This book was made possible by the support of Joomlashack.

We use Joomlashack extensions and templates to power all our Joomla sites.

The Joomlashack team built some of the most popular Joomla extensions in the world, including these:

- **OSMap** is a sitemap extension and will improve your SEO by helping Google find your site's content.
- **JCal Pro** is an awesome Joomla events calendar.
- **OSEmbed** allows you to embed anything in Joomla! With only the URL, you can easily share Twitter, Facebook, Instagram and other content.
- **OSCampus** is the best way to build an online training site with Joomla.

Check them out at http://joomlashack.com.

ABOUT THE OSTRAINING EVERYTHING CLUB

Multilingual Joomla Explained is part of the OSTraining Everything Club.

The club gives you access to all of the video classes, plus all the "Explained" books from OSTraining.

- These books are always up-to-date. Because we self-publish, we can release constant updates.

- These books are active. We don't do long, boring explanations.

- You don't need any experience. The books are suitable even for complete beginners.

Join the OSTraining Everything Club today by visiting our website at https://ostraining.com. You'll be able to download ebook copies of "Multilingual Joomla Explained" and all our other books and videos.

ABOUT THE OSTRAINING TEAM

Igor Mihaljko works full time for an IT company in Croatia as a Business Solutions Consultant. He is also passionate about Joomla and has been working with it since the beginning. He continues to work with Joomla in his spare time as a freelance Joomla developer. He also provides support for Joomla and writes blog posts about Joomla and documentation for various Joomla extensions. Igor works and lives in Zagreb, the capital city of Croatia, together with his wife Martina and two beautiful kids, Petra and Dino. You can contact Igor via his website https://mihha-vision.com.

Stephen Burge has split his career between teaching and web development. In 2007, he combined the two by starting to teach web development. His company, OSTraining, now teaches classes around the world and online. Stephen is originally from England and now lives in Florida.

WE OFTEN UPDATE THIS BOOK

This is version 1.0.0 of Multilingual Joomla Explained.

Multilingual Joomla Explained was first released in August 2017.

We aim to keep this book up-to-date, and so we will regularly release new versions to keep up with changes in Joomla.

If you find anything that is out-of-date, please email us at books@ostraining.com. We'll update the book, and to say thank you, we'll provide you with a new copy.

ADVANTAGES AND DISADVANTAGES

We often release updates for this book. Most of the time, frequent updates are wonderful. If Joomla makes a change in the morning, we can have a new version of this book available in the afternoon. Most traditional publishers wait years and years before updating their books.

There are two disadvantages to be aware of:

- Page numbers do change. We often add and remove material from the book to reflect changes in Joomla.
- There's no index at the back of this book. This is because page numbers do change, and also because our self-publishing platform doesn't have a way to create indexes yet. We hope to find a solution for that soon.

Hopefully, you think that the advantages outweigh the disadvantages. If you have any questions, we're always happy to chat: books@ostraining.com.

ARE YOU AN AUTHOR?

If you enjoy writing about the web, we'd love to talk with you.

Most publishing companies are slow, boring, inflexible and don't pay very well.

Here at OSTraining, we try to be different:

- **Fun**: We use modern publishing tools that make writing books as easy as blogging.
- **Fast**: We move quickly. Some books get written and published in less than a month.
- **Flexible**: It's easy to update your books. If technology changes in the morning, you can update your book by the afternoon.
- **Fair**: Profits from the books are shared 50/50 with the author.

Do you have a topic you'd love to write about? We publish books on almost all web-related topics.

Whether you want to write a short 100-page overview, or a comprehensive 500-page guide, we'd love to hear from you.

Contact us via email: books@ostraining.com.

ARE YOU A TEACHER?

Many schools, colleges and organizations have adopted our books as a teaching guide.

This book is designed to be a step-by-step guide that students can follow at different speeds. The book can be used for a one-day class, or a longer class over multiple weeks.

If you are interested in teaching Joomla, we'd be delighted to help you with review copies, and all the advice you need.

Please email books@ostraining.com to talk with us.

SPONSORING AN OSTRAINING BOOK

Is your company interested in sponsoring an OSTraining book?

Our books are some of the world's best-selling guides to the software they cover.

People love to read our books and learn about new web design topics.

Why not reach those people? Partner with us to showcase your company to thousands of web developers.

We have partnered with Acquia, Pantheon, Nexcess, GoDaddy, InMotion, GlowHost and Ecwid to provide sponsored training to millions of people.

If you want to learn more, visit https://ostraining.com/sponsor or email us at books@ostraining.com.

WE WANT TO HEAR FROM YOU

Are you satisfied with your purchase of Multilingual Joomla Explained? Let us know and help us reach others who would benefit from this book.

We encourage you to share your experience. Here are two ways you can help:

- Leave your review on Amazon's product page of Multilingual Joomla Explained.

- Email your review to books@ostraining.com.

Thanks for reading Multilingual Joomla Explained. We wish you the best in your future endeavors with Joomla.

THE LEGAL DETAILS

MULTILINGUAL JOOMLA EXPLAINED

Your Step-by-Step Guide to Building Multilingual Joomla Sites

IGOR MIHALJKO

STEPHEN BURGE

OSTraining
Bradenton

CONTENTS

CHAPTER 1.

INTRODUCING JOOMLA MULTILINGUAL SITES

We're going to show you how to create Joomla sites with content in multiple languages.

By the time you finish this book, you'll have a clear understanding of how to build multilingual Joomla sites. We're going to give you a complete walkthrough of the steps involved in the translation process.

But, before we begin, there are some key questions to answer:

- What do multilingual sites look like?
- Can I trust Joomla with my multilingual site?
- Are there any advantages or disadvantages to multilingual sites?

In this chapter, we'll answer those questions. Let's start by seeing some examples of real multilingual Joomla sites.

WHAT DOES A MULTILINGUAL SITE LOOK LIKE?

Joomla really can build professional-quality multilingual sites. Don't believe it? Let's look at some high-profile examples.

One of the most famous car companies in the world runs a

multilingual Joomla site. The site is at http://peugeot.com. Here's the English version:

In the bottom-right corner of the site, you can switch between Spanish, English and French:

The next image shows the French version. You can see that the site looks almost identical, except all the text is in French:

The internationally famous swimmer Michael Phelps also has a multilingual Joomla site that you can see at http://michaelphelps.com.

In the top-right corner of the site, you can use the flag icon to change the language of the site:

This next image shows the French version of the site. This time the French site is similar, but there are differences in the design and the content.

A multilingual site does not have to be English-first. https://medeor.de is a non-profit organization in Germany, and if you visit their site, you'll see content in German, as shown below:

In the top-right corner of the site, you'll see a link that says "English":

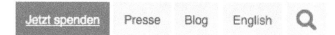

Click the "English" link, and you'll see the whole site has now been translated:

ADVANTAGES AND DISADVANTAGES OF MULTILINGUAL SITES

Before you decide to build a multilingual site, it is worth thinking about whether it's worth the time and effort.

On the positive side, there are many reasons why you would want a multilingual website:

- **The Web is Becoming Multilingual:** The internet began as an English speaker's invention and as a result, was dominated by English speaking users and sites. However, times are changing. As the world moves online, and internet access is available from Nigeria to Nanjing, English speakers will soon be in the minority when it comes to internet use.

- **Marketing:** Ultimately, a multilingual website is a marketing tool. By having your site accessible to more people, you are showcasing your company to more customers.

- **Customer-Focused:** A multilingual website demonstrates that you are thinking about the customer. That little extra effort shows you have thought and cared enough about them to offer the website in their language. As with anything in business, if the customer thinks you care, they will more likely want to do business with you.

- **Trust:** For many cultures, there is an issue of trust when it comes to buying over the internet, especially if they feel it is in a language they are not fully proficient in. Offering them a language alternative allows the customers to feel secure in the fact they know what they are buying, how they are buying it and who they are buying it from.

- **Culturally Sensitive:** A multilingual website, if designed properly, overcomes potential cultural barriers through allowing access in a native language. This automatically puts the user in a cultural comfort zone due to their being able to navigate, understand and interact with the website.

- **Competition:** Look at your competitors – if they have multilingual websites, then why don't you? If they don't, then why not lead the marketplace and establish your company or brand abroad before they do?

However, being realistic, there are some real disadvantages that come with multilingual sites:

- **Additional Complexity:** A multilingual website is more complex than a unilingual website. You will have to invest more to build and maintain your site's technical capabilities. Even apparently simple things, such as fonts and dates, can become tricky as you jump between different languages.

- **Initial Investment:** Your website will not create the translations for you. You will need to create the translations yourself or hire someone to do it for you. It may cost around $1,000 to translate 10,000 words.

- **Ongoing Investment**: Websites need updating, and you'll need to make plans to keep all the languages on your site up-to-date. You may also need to add customer support in more than one language.

A multilingual website is a very valuable asset for many organizations. But, it is not the right choice for everyone. Before choosing to build a multilingual site, sit down and think carefully about your budget, resources and goals.

WHAT'S NEXT?

So, you've considered the advantages and disadvantages, and you decided to build a multilingual site.

The next step is to choose the right approach for your site.

Look again at the website examples in this chapter, and you'll see that there is more than one way to build a multilingual site. The Peugeot site uses small text links to allow users to change the language: ES, EN and FR. Michael Phelps' site uses flags to represent each language. The Action Medeor site provides a simple link that says either English or Deutsch. If we looked deeper, we'd see many other differences between those sites as well.

In the next chapter, we'll review three of the most common approaches to building multilingual sites. This should help you decide which approach is the best match for you.

Turn the page and let's take an in-depth look at the different ways you can build a multilingual site.

CHAPTER 2.

DIFFERENT APPROACHES TO MULTILINGUAL JOOMLA

In this chapter, we're going to review different approaches to building multilingual sites.

There are many different ways to build a multilingual Joomla site, but these are three of the most common:

- **Approach #1:** Use Joomla's core features
- **Approach #2:** Use different websites for each language
- **Approach #3:** Replace Joomla's core features with a third party extension

In this book, we'll focus on Approach #1. However, this choice is not always straightforward, so in this chapter, we'll take a close look at all three approaches.

APPROACH #1: USE JOOMLA'S CORE FEATURES

You can build multilingual sites using a simple install of Joomla. By default, the Joomla core provides all the translation features you need.

If you choose this approach, you'll end up with a single website on a single domain name. A good example is https://joomla.org/3/. If you change the language, you will change the URL, but you will not move to a different domain name. For example, the German translation of this page is at https://joomla.org/3/de/, and the Spanish translation is at https://joomla.org/3/es/.

Using the Joomla core features and components to build a multilingual site on a single domain is the approach we recommend.

Here are the advantages of this solution:

- **Familiarity:** You will be using the normal Joomla administrator area. This should reduce the learning curve for your team.

- **Cost:** Since Joomla is free, you don't have to spend money to buy additional extensions which would provide multilingual features and translations.

Here are the disadvantages of this approach:

- **Extensions:** This approach may be difficult if you use a lot of extensions. Because not all of those extensions may be translated into all the languages you are using, you may have to translate the extensions yourself.

- **Less Flexibility:** This method won't work well if you have different requirements or need different features for each language. This approach requires that all your content be translated into each language.

APPROACH #2: USE DIFFERENT WEBSITES FOR EACH LANGUAGE

Using different domains for each language can be a valid choice, especially if you have a dedicated team who will be responsible for each website.

If you choose this option, you'll end up with a different website for each language. One example is the Nintendo family of websites in Scandinavia. The Swedish site is at https://nintendo.se, and that's shown in the image below. There's also a Danish version at https://nintendo.dk and a Finnish version at https://www.nintendo.fi. Notice that the domain name is different for each language. Also, the content is similar but is not identical in each language.

Here are the advantages of this approach:

- **Good for Multiple Teams:** If your organization is split into regional teams, having separate sites allows them more freedom. Allowing for regional variations could allow your staff to adapt more effectively to local needs.

- **More Flexibility:** Each website can have different features and different content. You don't have to require that your websites look identical in each language.

Here are the disadvantages of this approach:

- **Complexity:** Having multiple sites does make some things more difficult to implement. For example, imagine having a community area on your site for people to discuss issues. If you have multiple websites on different domains, you will have multiple community areas. Each community area will need to be configured and maintained, with few possibilities for integration.

- **Branding:** If you want to keep a consistent look-and-feel across each site, you will still need to impose standards on each site. Without close supervision, each site could quickly end up looking very different from the others.

So, why are we not going to talk more about Approach #2 in this book? Simply because there's not much to say. If you want to take this approach, you build several normal Joomla websites. That's it. You don't need a multilingual Joomla site. You just need multiple unilingual Joomla sites.

APPROACH #3: REPLACE JOOMLA'S CORE FEATURES WITH A THIRD PARTY EXTENSION

A third approach is to use a third-party extension for your multilingual site. Perhaps the most popular choice is Falang, which you can find at https://extensions.joomla.org/extension/falang/.

Here are the advantages of this approach:

- **Flexibility:** A non-core extension has more freedom to innovate than the Joomla core. Whereas the Joomla core already has a large base of users and can't change quickly, a non-core developer can design a whole new experience.

- **Faster Bug Fixes:** It is easier and quicker to fix the bugs in the non-core extension than in the Joomla core. Third-party developers usually react quickly to the bug reports and can push out new releases whenever they find a bug.

Here are the disadvantages of this approach:

- **Cost:** Usually, non-core extensions provide a limited set of features for free. More advanced features or support for other third-party extensions need to be purchased.

- **Learning Curve:** Non-core extensions can have an additional learning curve and can often do things in a completely different way than the Joomla core.

- **Reliance on the Developer:** You are relying on a single developer or a small team. The Joomla core is maintained by a large group of developers, and there is very little chance that progress will stop. However, it's not uncommon for non-core developers to go out of business.

WHAT'S NEXT?

In this chapter, we've seen that there are several different approaches to building multilingual Joomla sites.

In the rest of this book, we're going to a focus on Approach #1. We are going to build a multilingual website using a single domain and only the core Joomla features and components.

Are you ready? Turn the page, and let's start building your multilingual Joomla site.

CHAPTER 3.

INSTALLING A NEW MULTILINGUAL JOOMLA SITE

In this chapter, we show you how to install a brand new multilingual Joomla site.

If you already have a unilingual Joomla site and want to add another language, skip this chapter. You should read the next chapter, "Updating an Existing Unilingual Site".

In this chapter, you will learn:

• The best place to install Joomla

• The best way to install a multilingual Joomla site

CHOOSING THE BEST PLACE TO INSTALL JOOMLA

Joomla is not like many other software programs. It can't just run on any computer. It requires a server in order to run successfully. That means you normally have the choice of installing Joomla in one of two places:

• A local server installed on your computer

• A web server

Choosing the best place to install Joomla is important, so here is an explanation of the difference between the two options.

Your Computer

There are several useful advantages to working on your computer:

- **Working offline:** You can work without an internet connection.
- **Privacy:** Your Joomla site will be safe and private, accessible only to people who can access that computer.
- **Free:** There are no fees to pay.

However, there are also several important disadvantages to using a computer:

- **Extra installations needed:** You need to download and configure special software for your computer.
- **Difficult to get help:** You can't easily show it to other people and ask for help.
- **Only one computer:** You can only access it from the computer you used to install it.
- **Need to move in order to launch:** When you're ready to make your site public, you'll need to move everything to a web server and adjust for any differences between the two locations.

Because of these disadvantages, installing on your computer can present significant obstacles for a beginner. I'm going to recommend that you don't take this route until you have more experience.

A Web Server

Unlike your computer, a web server is specifically designed for hosting websites so they are easy to visit for anyone who's online.

If you work for a company, they may be able to provide a server. However, for most of us we'll need to rent space from a hosting company. There are two common types of web servers, Linux and Microsoft. Both require PHP, because that is the language Joomla is written in, and MySQL, because it is the type of database Joomla uses. These are the minimum versions recommended:

- **PHP**: 5.6 or above.
- **MySQL**: 5.5.3 or above.

Linux servers also require Apache, a type of web server software. The minimum version for that is 2 and above.

When it comes to choosing a server, Apache has long been the favorite choice for running Joomla. Microsoft is working hard to make Joomla run as smoothly as possible on their servers, but for now, Apache is still my recommendation.

Most hosting companies support Joomla, but it's worth choosing carefully. Some hosting companies are much better than others. Here is some advice before picking your host:

- Search http://forum.joomla.org for other people's experiences with that host.

- Contact their customer support and ask them what they know about Joomla. One of our training students actually called the phone numbers of several hosts and timed their responses. After all, in an emergency you don't want to be on hold for an hour or talking to someone who knows nothing about Joomla.

- Check prices. Most good hosting companies will charge around $6 to $10 per month for approximately 1 GB of space (enough for a 2000 page site) and 50 GB of bandwidth (enough for about 100,000 visitors per month).

CHOOSING THE BEST WAY TO INSTALL JOOMLA

For people who choose to install Joomla on a web server, there are two common ways to install Joomla:

- Use a "One-Click" installation.
- Upload the files and create the database manually.

The "One-Click" installation method is the fastest and easiest way to install Joomla. This method is done through a control panel such as those offered by Fantastico, Softaculous, cPanel and Plesk.

We do recommend that you install Joomla multilingual sites manually. This is because the "One-Click" installation methods don't support the creation of multilingual sites.

This means that you'll be moving Joomla files to the web server. For that, we'll need FTP (File Transfer Protocol) software. One good choice is Filezilla, which is free to download and can work on Windows, Mac or Linux computers. To download it, go to http://filezilla-project.org and click on "Download Filezilla Client".

HOW TO INSTALL A MULTILINGUAL JOOMLA SITE

An old-fashioned HTML website consists only of one part: files. It doesn't need anything else to run.

However, a Joomla website is a little different because it consists not only of files but also a database to store all the site's information. We're going to have to set-up both the files and the database, then connect them together. So, the process of installing Joomla manually is this:

- Step #1: Create a database

- Step #2: Download the Joomla files and upload them to our web server
- Step #3: Complete the Joomla installation by connecting the database and files together

Our first step will be to create a database to store all the unique information about our site.

A database is basically a group of tables with letters and numbers stored in its rows and columns. Think of it as several spreadsheets. There's a spreadsheet with all of the articles you write. There's another for all of the users who register on your site. The database makes it easy for Joomla to easily handle large amounts of data. If a new article or user is added, Joomla just needs to add an extra row to the appropriate spreadsheet. Joomla uses a particular type of database known as MySQL.

Let's go ahead and set up a database for our new Joomla site:

- Log in to your web hosting account. In this example, we're using a web hosting control panel called CPanel, as provided by a hosting company called Siteground.com. Their version of CPanel looks like the image below. Your hosting company may offer a slightly different version of CPanel, or they may offer an alternative that looks a little different but works in a very similar way.

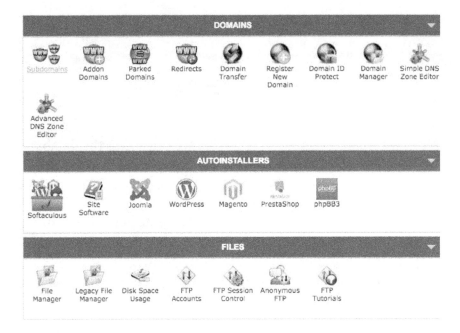

- Find the button that says "MySQL Databases" (as seen on the far left of the screen below) and click it. The button may be on any of the rows, but you can normally spot it by looking for the MySQL name and the blue dolphin logo.

- Enter a name that is relatively easy to remember and click "Create Database". Be sure to write this name down, and note that it's likely to have your hosting account name before it. In the image below, our new database will be called ostrain2_joomlaville.

Create a New Database

New Database: ostrain2_ joomlaville ✓

Create Database

Next, we create a user account so that we can access the database. Without password protection, anyone might be able to log in and see our site's important information. Here's what you need to do:

- Choose a username. Enter a short username here, different from anything you've used before. In this example, I'm using "joomlav". The username is a little confusing because our hosting account name is added also, so in the image below, our full username will be ostrain2_joomlav.

- Choose a password. Some versions of CPanel will help you choose a password that is very difficult to guess. If you set your own choice, please use a combination of numbers, punctuation and uppercase and lowercase letters so that the password is hard to guess.

- Be sure to record both your username and password safely. We're going to need them again very soon.

- Click "Create User". You should see a message saying the user has been created successfully.

MySQL Users

Add a New User

Username: ostrain2_ joomlav ✓

Password: •••••••••••••••••• ✓

Password (Again): •••••••••••••••••• ✓

Strength (Why?): Very Strong (100/100) Password Generator

Create a User

Now we need to allow our new user to be able to login to the database.

- Find the area called "Add User To Database".

- Choose your database name and then your username before clicking "Add".

Add a User to a Database

User: ostrain2_joomlav ⬍

Database: ostrain2_joomlaville ⬍

Add

- **The final step in this process is to decide what our new user can and cannot do with the database. As in the image below, we're going to give them "All" permissions so that our Joomla site can make whatever changes it needs to the database. Click on "Make Changes"" to finish the process:**

Manage User Privileges

User: **ostrain2_joomlav**
Database: **ostrain2_joomlaville**

☑ ALL PRIVILEGES	
☑ ALTER	☑ ALTER ROUTINE
☑ CREATE	☑ CREATE ROUTINE
☑ CREATE TEMPORARY TABLES	☑ CREATE VIEW
☑ DELETE	☑ DROP
☑ EVENT	☑ EXECUTE
☑ INDEX	☑ INSERT
☑ LOCK TABLES	☑ REFERENCES
☑ SELECT	☑ SHOW VIEW
☑ TRIGGER	☑ UPDATE

Make Changes

Step #2: Download the Joomla Files

Now that we have the database ready, we're going to download the Joomla files. These contain all of the code and images that Joomla needs to run.

- Go to http://joomla.org and click on the button saying "Download Joomla!".

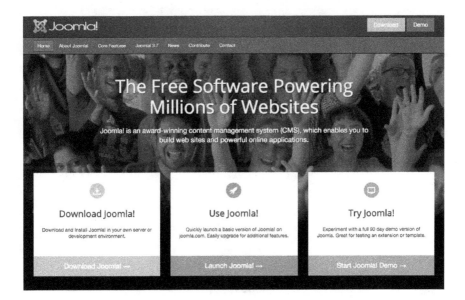

- You'll now see a page with several download links. Click the "Download Joomla!" button on the left.

- After clicking the download link, you'll receive a .zip file with a name like this: Joomla_3.8.5-Stable-Full_Package.zip. It contains all the files you'll need to install Joomla.

- Now you need to uncompress the .zip file. On a Windows computer, you can right-click on the file and choose "Extract

Here". On a Mac, if the file doesn't unzip automatically, you can click on "File" then "Open With" and choose "Archive Utility". The folder will have a name similar to Joomla_3.8.5-Stable-Full_Package. Right-click on the folder and rename it to /joomlaville/.

- Open the folder, and the contents will look like this:

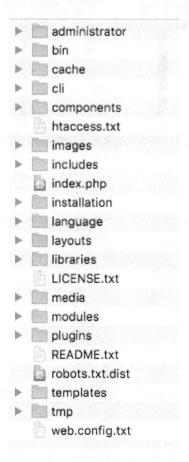

We're now going to start the process of moving our files on to our web server.

- The first step is to open your FTP software such as Filezilla. Then log in to your FTP account and browse to the folder where you want to install Joomla. Often this will be the root directory, which often has a name such as /public_html/, /www/ or /htdocs/.

- Select the folder that you just downloaded, extracted and renamed. Move this folder via your FTP software into the folder where you're installing Joomla. With Filezilla this is as simple as dragging-and-dropping the files. Uploading might take from 5 to 30 minutes or more depending on the speed of your internet connection.

Step #3: Complete the Joomla Installation

We've now successfully set up the two halves of our Joomla site: the database (Step #1) and the files (Step #2). Our final step is to connect those two halves together.

- Start your browser and visit the URL where you uploaded the files. In the example I've been using, that was to http://ostraining.com/joomlaville/.
- You should see an installation screen like the figure below. This is the first step in Joomla's easy-to-use installation manager.

Enter the information listed here, and then click the "Next" button:

- Site Name: **Multilingual Joomla**
- Admin Email: Enter your email address.
- Admin Username: Enter the username you want to use when you log in to your site.
- Admin Password: This is the password you'll use to log in. Please don't use "admin" here also! Don't use "password", "1234" or "iloveyou" either. A good combination of numbers, punctuation and uppercase and lowercase letters is vital.

After clicking "Next", you will be asked for your database details. This is where you connect your files and database together. We're going to need the details we collected when we created the database earlier. Enter the information we list here, and then click the "Next" button.

- Username: Enter the details you collected earlier.

- Password: Enter the details you collected earlier.

- Database Name: Enter the details you collected earlier.

Next, let's install some sample data so that our site is ready to use straight away. In the options below, choose "Brochure English", as shown in the image below:

- Install Sample Data: Choose **Brochure English**. This is going to give us some basic English pages that we can work with and translate into French. Don't worry if you skip this step or make the wrong choice. You are still going to be able to follow along throughout the next chapters without any problems.

After you click on the blue "Install" button, Joomla is going to install your website. If you are building a multilingual Joomla website, the most important step is going to come on the next screen, after this installation process has finished.

Normally, you would click on the "Remove installation folder" button to finish the installation process. However, we need to take a different approach for our multilingual site.

- Go and click on the blue button with the title "Extra steps: Install languages".

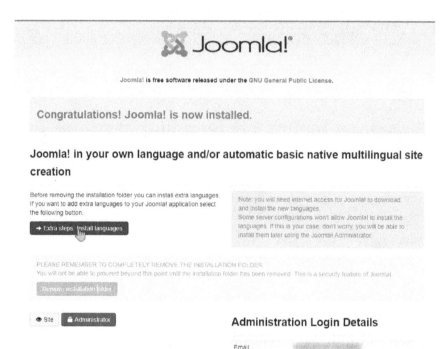

You now get a choice of all the different languages that are available for Joomla: Afrikaans, Albanian, Croatian, all the way down in the alphabetical order.

Joomla!

Joomla! is free software released under the GNU General Public License.

1 Install Languages   2 Choose Default Language   3 Finish

Install Language packages

← Previous   → Next

The Joomla interface is available in several languages. Choose your preferred languages by choosing the checkboxes and then install them by selecting the Next button.

Note: this operation will take about 10 seconds to download and install every language. To avoid timeouts please select no more than 3 languages to install.

Language	Language Tag	Version
Afrikaans	af-ZA	3.7.2.1
Albanian	sq-AL	3.4.4.2
Arabic Unitag	ar-AA	3.7.2.1
Armenian	hy-AM	3.4.4.1
Bahasa Indonesia	id-ID	3.6.2.1
Basque	eu-ES	3.7.2.1
Belarusian	be-BY	3.2.1.2
Bosnian	bs-BA	3.6.3.1
Bulgarian	bg-BG	3.6.5.2
Catalan	ca-ES	3.7.0.1
Chinese Simplified	zh-CN	3.4.1.2
Chinese Traditional	zh-TW	3.7.6.2
Croatian	hr-HR	3.8.5.1
Czech	cs-CZ	3.8.5.1
Danish	da-DK	3.7.2.1
Dari Persian	prs-AF	3.4.4.2
Dutch	nl-NL	3.7.2.1
Dzongkha	dz-BT	3.6.2.1
English AU	en-AU	3.8.5.1
English CA	en-CA	3.8.5.1
English NZ	en-NZ	3.8.5.1

Don't worry too much if you see the message saying "Language pack does not match this Joomla version. Some strings may be missing". Despite this message, it is likely that you are going to have 98% or 99% of the language you need and maybe just one or two tiny items are missing.

- We are building a website in English and French, so click on the "French" box.

- Scroll up to the top and click on "Next".

1. Install Languages   2. Choose Default Language   3. Finish

Install Language packages

← Previous   → Next

Next

The Joomla interface is available in several languages. Choose your preferred languages by choosing the checkboxes and then install them by selecting the Next button.
Note: this operation will take about 10 seconds to download and install every language. To avoid timeouts please select no more than 3 languages to install.

Language	Language Tag	Version
Afrikaans	af-ZA	3.7.2.1
Albanian	sq-AL	3.1.1.2
Arabic Unitag	ar-AA	3.7.2.1
Armenian	hy-AM	3.4.4.1
Bahasa Indonesia	id-ID	3.8.2.1
Basque	eu-ES	3.7.2.1
Belarusian	be-BY	3.2.1.2
Bosnian	bs-BA	3.9.5.1
Bulgarian	bg-BG	3.8.5.2
Catalan	ca-ES	3.7.0.1
Chinese Simplified	zh-CN	3.4.1.2
Chinese Traditional	zh-TW	3.7.8.2
Croatian	hr-HR	3.8.5.1
Czech	cs-CZ	3.6.5.1
Danish	da-DK	3.7.2.1

- In the "Default Administrator language" and "Default Site language" areas, choose the primary language for your site. This will be the default language that users see when they login, although they will quickly be able to choose a different language.

- Click **Yes** for "Activate the multilingual feature".
- Click **Yes** for "Install localized content".
- Click **Yes** for "Enable the language code plugin".

This language code plugin is important because it will create different URLs for different languages. For example, all the English pages may start with "en" in the URL. All the French pages may start with "fr" in the URL:

- http://example.com/en/about
- http://example.com/fr/faites-notre

This enables us to keep a clean organization of the URLs on our site.

At this point, we have nearly completed the installation process.

- Click on "Next", and you will be taken to the final page.
- Click on the "Remove installation folder" button.

- Click the "Site" button. You will be taken to visit your multilingual site.

Look at your new site. You will notice several things:

- In the top right corner, there is a French flag and an English flag, already setup and already created for us.

- The default language of the site is English, although there is also some dummy content in Latin.
- Some of the English items are marked en-GB which means that the British version of English is being used.

- Click on the French flag in the top-right corner.

Notice how you can move back-and-forth between the French and English version of the site. As you change between English and French, you will see that that "en" and "fr" are in the URL.

We have a multilingual site that is working successfully!

So, if you install a brand new Joomla site and choose the settings that we just did, it really is a big help in getting started with a multilingual Joomla site.

- Add the word "administrator" to your domain name so that you are visiting http://example.com/administrator.

- On the login screen, you will be presented with a language choice. If you login in English, you will be presented with an admin interface in the English language. However, if you login in French, you will be presented with an admin interface in French. The whole interface has been translated for you in French.

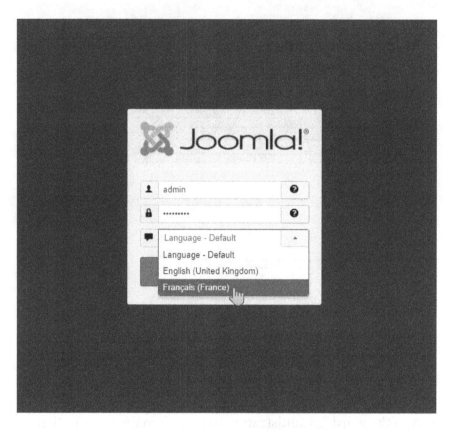

Take a look around at the French and English versions of the admin area. You may need to login and logout to change the language display. You'll see that the whole of the admin interface is successfully translated. You really now do have a good basis for building a multilingual site.

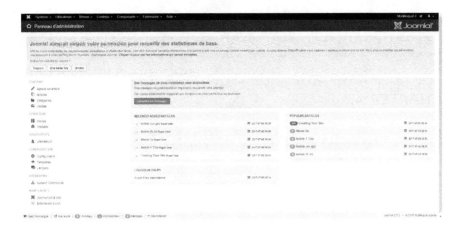

WHAT'S NEXT?

Because you successfully completed this chapter, you can skip the next chapter, "Updating an Existing Unilingual Site". That chapter is written for people who already have a site and need to translate it for the first time.

You can move directly to the chapter "Translating Joomla Articles", where we'll explain the process you'll use to translate content in Joomla.

CHAPTER 4.

UPDATING AN EXISTING UNILINGUAL SITE

In the previous chapter of this book, we showed you how to create a new multilingual Joomla website. This is the easiest method because Joomla does so many things automatically for you.

However, not all of us are going to be lucky enough to be in that situation. Some of you will need to translate an existing unilingual website. That is what we are going to cover in this chapter.

We are going to start with a normal Joomla website, and we're going to show you how to translate it into French. We're going to use this 5 step process:

1. Install a new language
2. Set up a content language
3. Enable the two language plugins
4. Publish the Language Switcher module
5. Set up the menus

STEP #1. INSTALL A NEW LANGUAGE

Our first step will be to install the new language for your Joomla site.

- Log into the administrator area for your Joomla site:

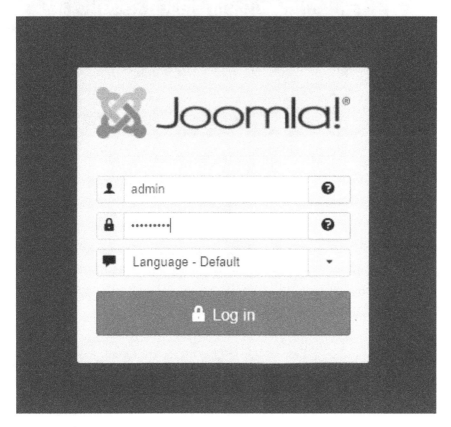

- Go to "Extensions", then "Language(s)":

- Click on the "Install Languages" button:

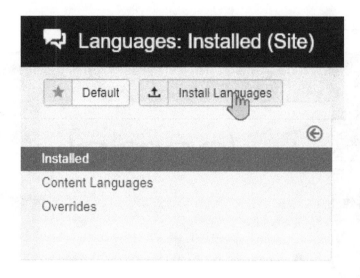

In this example, we're going to install the French language for our site. This process will install many of the language strings we need to complete the translation of our site.

- Search for "French":

- Click "Install" next to the French result, as shown on the screen below.

Don't worry if it says that the language pack doesn't match the Joomla version. In my experience (especially with more popular languages like French) all of the language strings you need are going to be there. This message may be showing because someone just hasn't tagged this language pack for the very latest release of Joomla.

- After a few moments, you will see a screen like the one below, which should tell you that the installation was successful:

STEP #2. ADD A CONTENT LANGUAGE

In this step, we're going to define the settings for the French content on our site.

- Go to "Extensions", "Language(s)" and then "Content Languages":

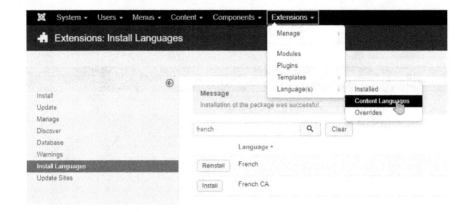

- At the moment, only English is set up with the details that we need:

- Click "New" in the top-left corner:

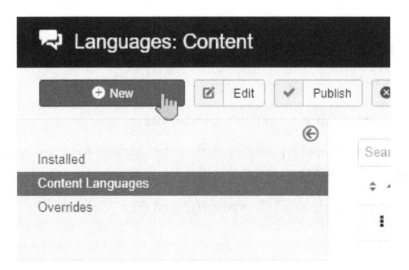

On this next screen, you can choose the flag, the settings, the URLs and other options for our French language.

- Title: **French (FR)**
- Title Native: **Français (France)**

Notice that these two settings are different. The Title box is the word for French according to the default language of the site, which in this case is English. The Title Native box is the word for French in French.

If someone is browsing the site in English, they are going to see French referred to as French (FR). If someone is browsing the site in French, they are going to see French referred to as Français (France).

It is not essential to put (FR) and (France) after the title, but that might help eliminate confusion for people who don't speak the version of French spoken in France. This is similar to the English (en-GB) setting that we saw earlier in the chapter.

- Language Tag: **fr-FR**

This is one of the trickier elements of this setup. We are going to use "fr-FR", but there are different possibilities here:

The lowercase "fr" is the way we refer to French.

The uppercase "FR" refers to the French language as is spoken in France. But, you can also have versions of French spoken in Canada, Belgium, Switzerland, and other countries. This site has a complete list of options: http://lingoes.net/en/translator/langcode.htm. For example, "en-GB" is the default for our site, but we can have "en-US" for American English, or "en-CA" for Canadian English. And then we have multiple possibilities for Spanish, different possibilities for Portuguese. These different variations of English and French use different words and different spellings, and so it is possible to enter different choices in this language tag.

- The "URL Language Code" field refers to the letters that are going into the URL. If we have a contact page in English, it is probably going to start with the letters "en" before the word "contact". If we have a contact page in French, "fr" is going to be our choice for the URL.

- "Image" is more simply known as the flag. We can choose whatever flag we want to represent French, although it may make more sense to choose the French flag. This is what people are going to see on the front end of the site when they click to change from one language to another.

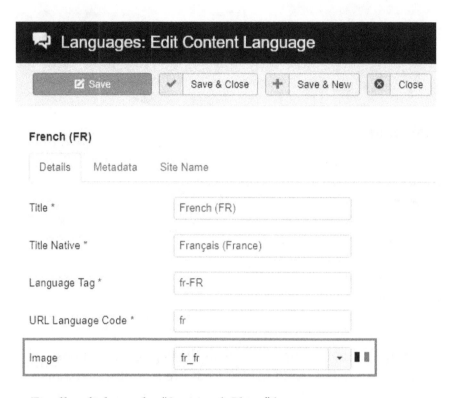

- Finally, click on the "Save and Close" button:

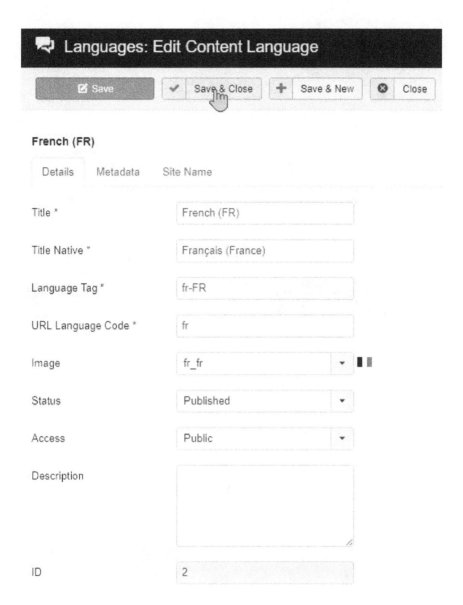

- You will see that French is now also listed as a content language:

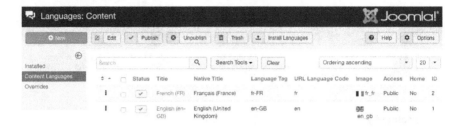

STEP #3. ENABLE THE TWO LANGUAGE PLUGINS

In this step, we enable two different plugins that will power the multilingual features of our site.

- Go to "Extensions", then "Plugins":

- One plugin is called "System – Language Filter". The other one is called "System – Language Code". Both of these can easily be found if we type "language" in the search box:

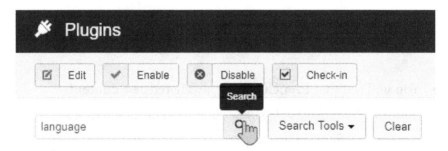

- Those were the only two plugins that came back when we searched for "language". We will enable both of them to complete Step #3 of the setup process!

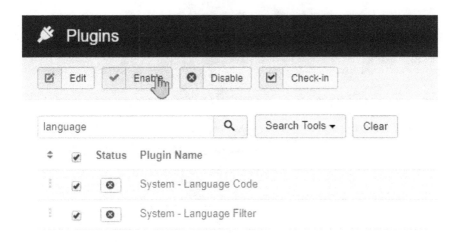

STEP #4. PUBLISH THE LANGUAGE SWITCHER MODULE

In this step, we are going to create a module that will show the language flags on the front end of the site.

- Go to " Extensions", and then "Modules":

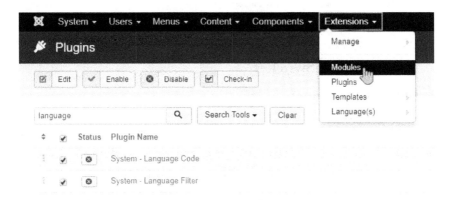

- The module we want doesn't exist yet, so click "New":

- Choose the "Language Switcher" module:

- Title: **Language Switcher**

- Position: **position-1**

Note that position-1 is the right sidebar area for the default Joomla template. If you are not using the default Joomla template, you may need to choose another position.

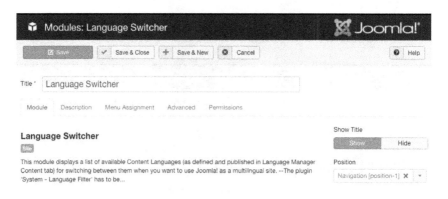

- Click on the "Save & Close" button:

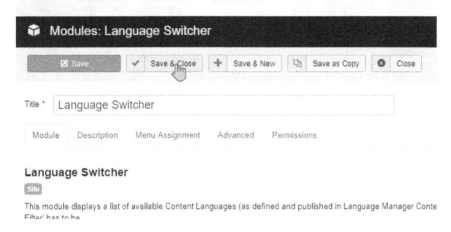

- Go to the front of the site and refresh the page. You should see your new module on the right-hand side:

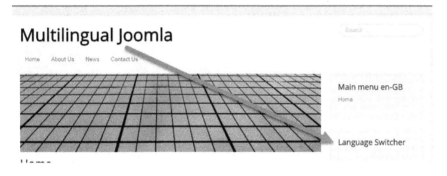

You can see the module but, oddly, it is blank. We can't actually see the flags yet. The reason that we can't see any flags is that we haven't actually defined any content as being specifically English or specifically French yet. That is going to be the fifth and final step in our process.

STEP #5. SET UP THE MENUS

- Go to the Joomla admin area.
- Go to "Menus", then go to "Manage" and "Add New Menu":

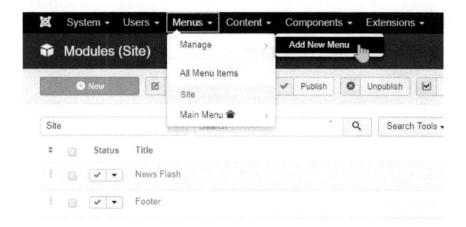

We are going to make a new menu specifically for our English content.

- Title: **English menu**
- Menu type: **english menu**

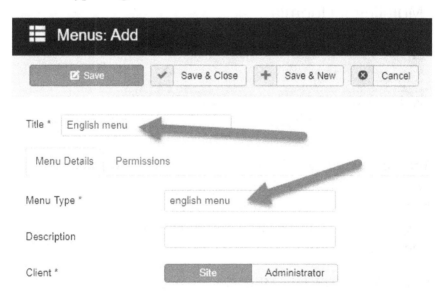

- Click the "Save and Close" button:

We are going to repeat the same process again because we also need to define a French menu for our French content.

- Click "New".
- Title: **French menu**
- Menu type: **french menu**
- Click "Save and Close".

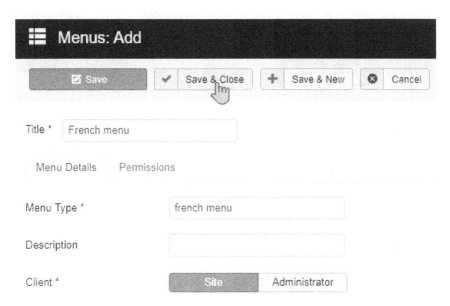

We now have three different menus. All of our English links are going to be put in the English menu. All of our French links will go into the French menu.

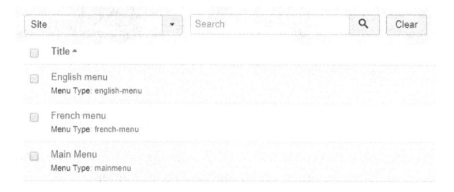

Now that we have an English menu, let's make an English homepage too.

- Go to "Menus", then "English menu" and finally "Add New Menu Item":

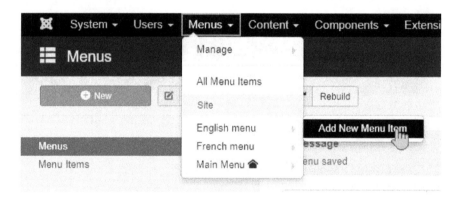

- Menu Title: **English Homepage**

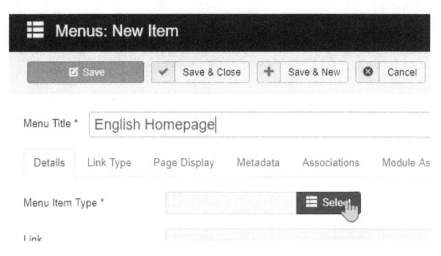

- Menu Item Type: Click "Articles" and choose "Featured Articles":

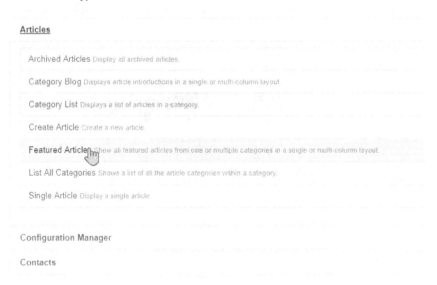

- Status: **Published**
- Default Page: **Yes**
- Language: **English (en-GB)**

- Click on "Save & Close":

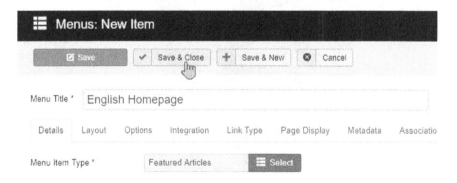

We now have an English homepage. You can tell it is actually our homepage because there is a British flag under the "Home" column. Normally we have a gold star in Joomla to mark the homepage. With multilingual sites, we have the language flag in order to indicate that this is a homepage for this particular language.

Now let's repeat that process and create a French homepage.

- Go to "Menus", then "French menu", and click "Add New Menu Item":

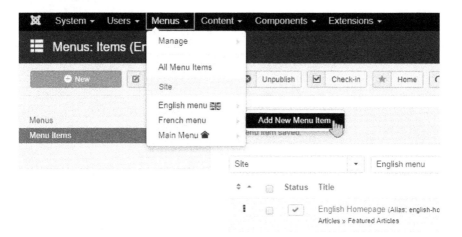

- Title: **French Homepage**
- Menu Item Type: **Featured Articles**
- Status: **Published**
- Default Page: **Yes**
- Language: **French (FR)**
- Click the "Save and Close" button.

- You should now see that your French homepage has the French flag next to it:

- If you go to the front of your site and refresh your homepage, you are going to see both flags that are now available in the Language Switcher module:

If you click on the French flag, you should see that some parts of the homepage are now translated into French:

- The Login Form now has French text.

- The URL now contains /fr/ We now are browsing a home page that has "fr" in the URL instead of "en".

- The breadcrumbs are now in French.

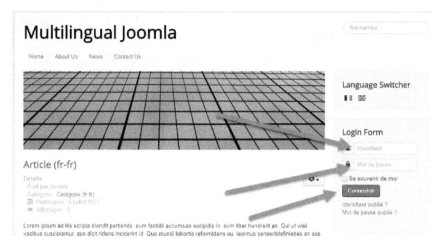

Let's click on the English flag to test it. The Login Form has turned back into English, the URL contains "en", and the breadcrumbs have also been translated into English.

Excellent! It appears that we have now gone through the five-step process and have successfully set up our multilingual site.

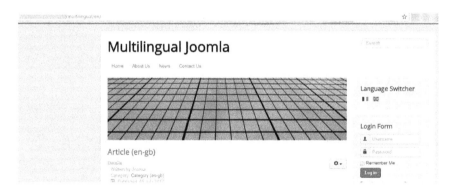

WHAT'S NEXT?

At this point, you have a site that can be called "multilingual". You can move back-and-forth from the French version of the site to the English version.

However, there are limits to what we've done so far. Much of the site's content remains untranslated.

In the next chapter, we'll start to translate your Joomla content. Turn the page, and let's dig in.

CHAPTER 5.

TRANSLATING JOOMLA ARTICLES

This is the part of the book where you start to translate your content.

At this point, you should already have installed a new multilingual site, or have modified an existing unilingual site. If you haven't done either of those things, please read the previous two chapters.

In this chapter, we are going to introduce you to "Associations", which are the key to building multilingual websites.

For this demonstration, we are going to use a new site, installed according to the process described in "Installing a new Multilingual Website". The website is partially translated into English and French. However, no matter what kind of multilingual website you have, you should be able to follow along with what we'll be doing in these chapters.

Let's take a look at the website that we have in front of us. We have a French and a British flag, and we can successfully toggle back and forth between the two.

Language Switcher

- When we click the French flag, the site translates into French:

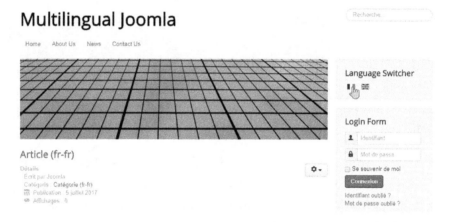

- When we click the British flag, the site goes back to English again:

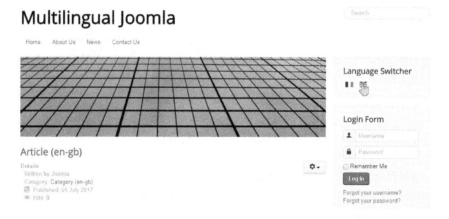

We have a working multilingual website, but you will notice that many things aren't being translated. If we move to French, you will notice that many elements on the page remain in English.

For example, the main menu is still in English and so are the module titles.

Many elements of the page haven't been translated yet, and that is what we are going to try to start to tackle in this chapter.

- Take a look at the homepage, and you will notice there is an article labelled "en-gb" for British English:

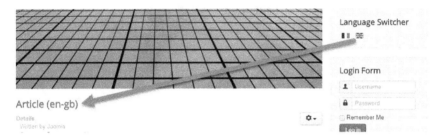

- We click the French flag, and it does change to the "fr-fr", the French version of the article:

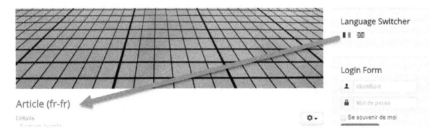

This is successfully translated because we do have a homepage for English and a homepage for French as well. On a normal Joomla website, the hompage would be marked by a gold star. In this situation, we have two homepages. One is marked with the French flag and one is marked with the British flag.

However, although the homepage is working correctly, many inside pages have problems.

- Click on the British flag.

- Click on "About Us", and you will see a page which is clearly in English:

- Click on the French flag.

- You are going to be bumped right back to the homepage. You can see from the URL that you have lost the page that you were on. You are no longer on any kind of "About Us" page. Joomla is saying that it doesn't have a French version of this "About Us" page, and so it breaks.

How do we fix the broken "About Us" page in French?

- Go to your Joomla admin area.

- Go to "Content" and then "Articles".

- Find the "About Us" article.

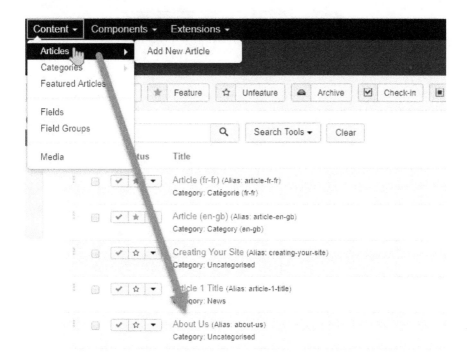

- Click on the title of the "About Us" article.

Let's make sure that Joomla knows exactly what language this article is in.

- On the right-hand side, you can see the language is set to "All".

- Click and make sure that "Language" is specifically set to "English (en-GB)".

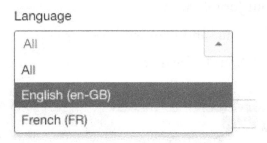

- The text in the main body of the article is a little short, so I am going to make it a little bit longer. Go to http://lipsum.com and copy-paste some dummy text into the article.

- Click "Save & Close".

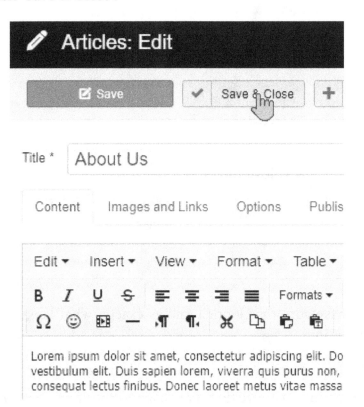

The "About Us" article is now successfully set up in the English version of the page. Look at the "Language" column on the right-hand side of the page and you can see that "About Us" is labelled as being English.

Now let's create a French version of this About Us article.

- Click on "New":

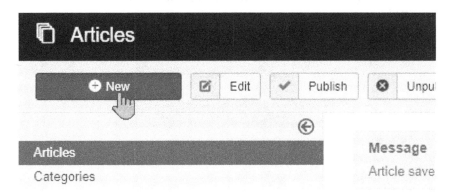

- Title: **À propos de nous**

- Content: Let's fill in the rest of the article to represent the French version of the article. For the ease of explanation, I am going to use "lorem ipsum" text here as well.

- On the right-hand side, under "Language", choose "French (FR)":

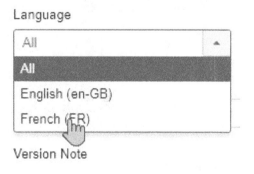

- Click on the "Associations" tab.

This is a very important feature of multilingual sites. Associations allow us to tell Joomla that we have an "About Us" article and this is the French version of it. This is going to make sure our multilingual site works successfully.

- Under the "Associations" tab , click on the "Select" button.
- Choose the English "About Us" article.

- After choosing "About Us", your screen will look like the image below. This is explicitly telling Joomla that these articles are translations of each other.

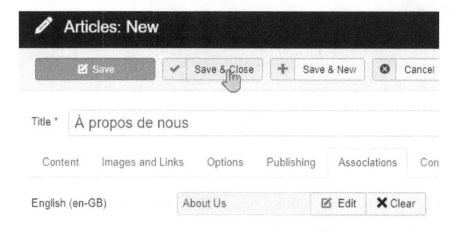

- Click "Save & Close", and you will see that change has taken place in the main article screen:

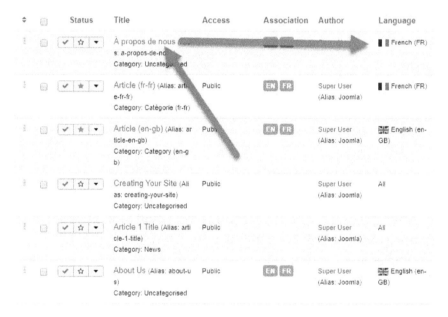

- "About Us" is now labelled as English and "À propos de nous" is labelled as French. There is now an "Association" column.

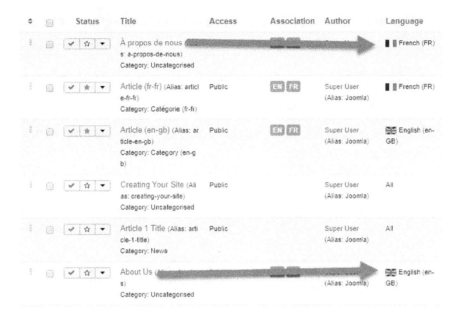

Joomla is telling you that these two articles are direct translations of each other. The Association column enables you to see which article it's a translation of.

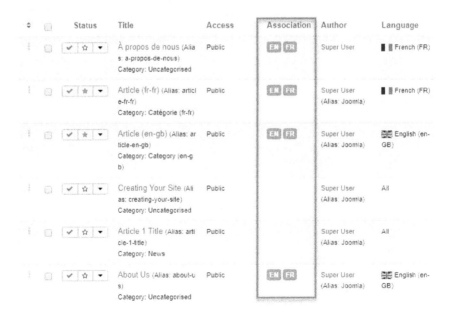

Now it's time to test that translation that we have set up. Let's see if the French version is working.

- Visit the front of your site and click "About Us" in the menu.
- Click the French flag.
- The title is translated, and the text in the article has changed as well.

You will notice that not only is the article itself translated, but also the URL is in French, as shown in the screen below. It includes the "fr" snippet that we set up, and it includes the French language version of the URL too.

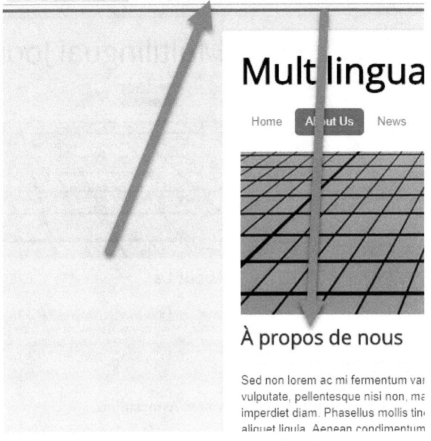

- Click on the British flag, and you are back to the English language version of the page:

/multilingual/en/about-us

Multilingual Joor

ome **About Us** News Contact Us

About Us

Lorem ipsum dolor sit amet, consectetur adipiscing
porttitor. Praesent augue orci, feugiat eget turpis eç
amet suscipit quis, sodales vestibulum elit. Duis sa

WHAT'S NEXT?

In this chapter, we introduced you to Associations.

Associations are going to be the key feature we use to translate
the rest of our site. During the next few chapters, we'll use
Associations to translate more of our site, including the
components, modules, categories, menus and more.

In the next chapter, we'll show you how to translate Joomla
menus and menu links. Turn the page, and let's translate our
menus and menu links.

CHAPTER 6.

TRANSLATING JOOMLA MENUS

In the previous chapter, we saw the power of Associations. We were able to link articles together so when the visitors clicked on the flags on the front end of our site, they were taken from one version of the article to another.

Click on the British flag, and you get the English version of the article. Click on the French flag, and you get the French version:

However, the process is not entirely complete yet. You will notice that even though we are looking at the French version, you still see "About Us" up in the main menu of the site. That is what we are going to fix in this chapter.

HOW TO TRANSLATE JOOMLA MENUS

Go to the admin area of the site and click "Menus". You will see that you have an English and a French menu set up.

We are going to use these menus to show different menu links to different visitors.

We're going to make the English menu visible when people are looking at our site in English. We're going to make the French menu visible when people are looking at our site in French.

- Go to "Extensions", then "Modules".

You will notice that there are three menu modules available.

- Main Menu: This is the menu that we have been looking at so far throughout the previous chapters.
- Main Menu en-GB
- Main Menu fr-FR

What we are going to do is unpublish the default Main Menu, because it is not needed in the English or French version of the site. Instead, we are going to put the English menu and the French menu up to the top, in the module area "position-1".

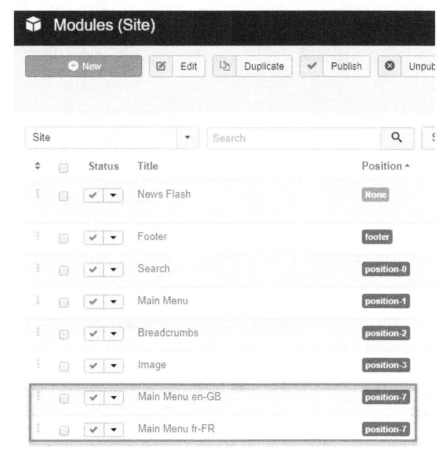

- Edit the "Main Menu en-GB" module.
- Position: **position-1**
- Click "Save & Close".

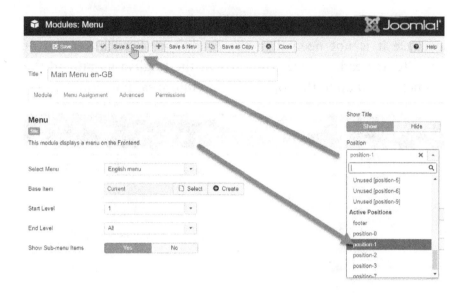

We need to repeat that process for the "Main Menu fr-FR" module as well.

- Edit the"Main Menu fr-FR" module and choose "position-1".
- Click "Save & Close".

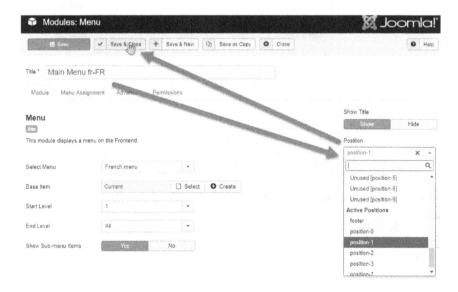

Now, if we visit the front of the site, we see that French viewers will see "Accueil" in the main menu bar and English viewers will see "Home".

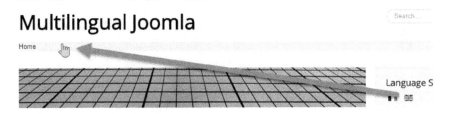

Multilingual Joomla

We are not 100% there because a little bit of design and a little bit of CSS is missing from the menu. Some of the default Main Menu settings are missing from our new menus.

- Go back to edit the "Main Menu en-GB" module.

- Click the "Advanced" tab.

- Menu Class Suffix: " nav-pills". Don't forget the extra space at the beginning.

- Module Class Suffix: remove "_menu" to leave this field blank.

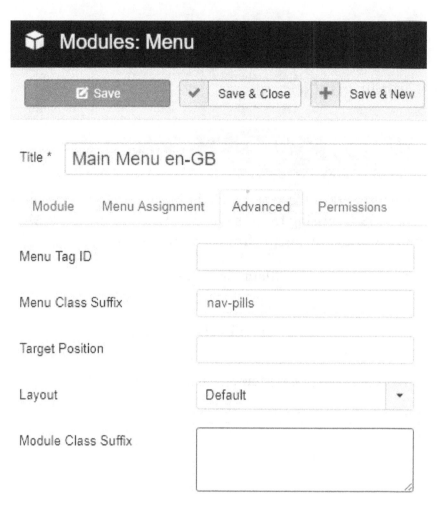

- Repeat the process for the French language menu.
- Remove "_menu" from the "Module Class Suffix" field and put " nav-pills" into the "Menu Class Suffix" field.

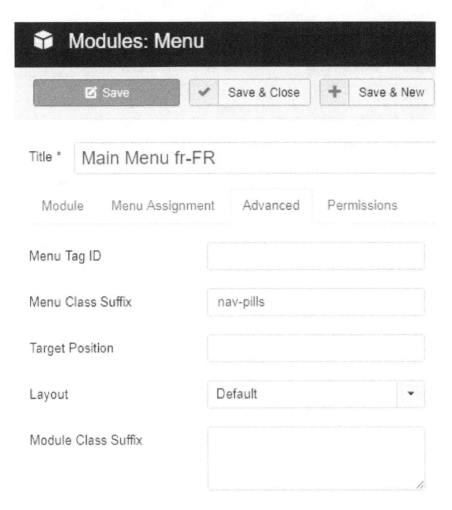

If we go back to the front of our site, you should see that rounded corners are now available for our menu links.

Multilingual Joomla

Click on the French flag, and you should now see that the menu has been successfully translated. Not only is the article in French, but the menu links are in French now too.

Multilingual Joomla

Accueil

Langua;
❚❚ 🏴

CREATING ASSOCIATION FOR MENUS

One thing you may be asking at this point is why we haven't done an Association?

That is a great question. It is not absolutely essential to have an Association for every single part of the site. You can see that the translation works without an Association for the menu. However, it only works because we have an association for the article already.

My advice is to try and use Associations wherever you possibly can. That will produce the smoothest effect for your users. There may be some times in which you don't actually have a version for the content in both languages. In that case, it is acceptable to skip it; but for now, I am going to recommend we create an association for our menu links too.

• Go back to "Menus" and the "English menu".

Notice that the "About Us" menu item does not have a specified language. This can cause confusion. For example, if you don't specify a language, you can click the "Associations" tab and choose both a French and English language version. To eliminate that confusion, we recommend that you get in the habit of always specifying the language when creating categories, articles, menu links and other items in Joomla.

Let's follow our own advice, and specify the language for this menu link:

• Click on the "Details" tab.

- Set the "Language" option to "English (en-GB)".
- Go back to the "Associations" tab. Make sure that Joomla is no longer offering us the ability to choose an English version of the menu link.
- Create an Association to the "À propos de nous" article, as shown in the image below.
- Click "Save & Close".

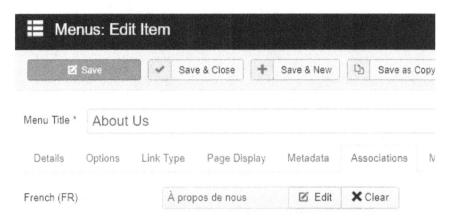

So, now we have an Association between "À propos de nous" and "About Us" at the article level and at the menu level as well.

That is going to produce the most reliable multilingual experience for our visitors.

WHAT'S NEXT?

We currently have an association between articles and menu links.

In the next chapter, we are going to take this a step further. We're going to create a French and an English version of a category, multiple articles and multiple menu links.

Rather than simply translating individual items, we're moving towards translating your whole site.

CHAPTER 7.

TRANSLATING A JOOMLA BLOG

During the last few chapters of this book, we have seen how to translate articles and menus.

We're going to take that a step further in this chapter, and we'll translate a whole area of our site. We're going to make a blog page for both our English and our French visitors.

Creating a blog is going to involve creating categories, articles and menu links, in both English and French. We will also associate them together using the techniques learned in the previous chapters. In addition to this, we'll add one extra piece of difficulty. We are going to create a "Latest News" module so people can see the latest blog posts that were added to the site.

Let's go through that process. By the time we are finished, you will have a much clearer understanding of the big picture that is involved in building a multilingual site.

CREATING MULTILINGUAL JOOMLA CATEGORIES

Our first step in creating a multilingual blog is to translate categories. This is the process we are going to use for categories:

- We'll make an English category.
- We'll make a French category.

- We'll associate the two categories together.

Let's see how that process works:

- Go to the admin area of your Joomla site.
- Go to "Content", and then "Categories":

- Click "New":

- Title: **Blog (en)**. As we explained earlier in the book, it's not essential to put (en) in here. But for the purpose of this book, using this tag will make it easier to identify the different languages.
- Language: **English (en-GB)**.

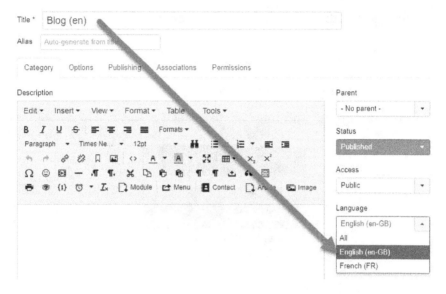

- Click on "Save & New":

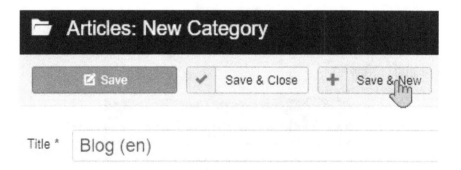

Now we're going to make the French version:

- Title: **Blog (fr)**
- Language: **French (FR)**

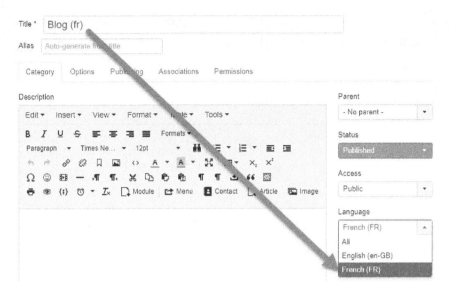

- Click on "Save". We don't want to close and exit the category screen yet.

- When the save has been processed, click on the "Associations" tab:

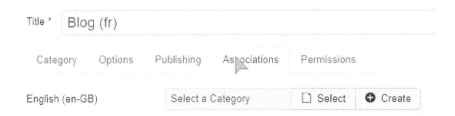

- We're going to link the two new categories. Click "Select a Category" and choose "Blog (en)":

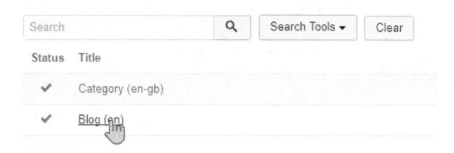

- Click "Save & Close":

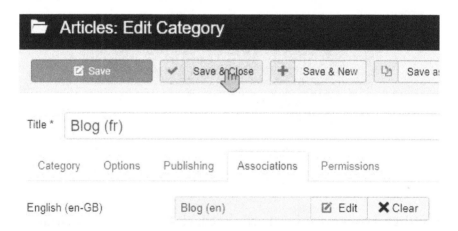

- We should now see that the two articles have the correct flags:

CREATING MULTILINGUAL JOOMLA ARTICLES

Our next step is to put some articles inside those two multilingual categories. We are going to use a very similar process to the one we used for categories:

- We'll make an English article.
- We'll make a French article.
- We'll associate the two articles together.

Let's start the article creation process:

- Go to "Content", and then "Articles":

- Cick on the "New" button:

- Title: **Blog article 1**
- Content: This text is taken from http://lipsum.com.

- Category: **Blog (en) (en-GB)**
- Language: **English (en-GB)**

- Click on "Save & New":

Title * Blog article 1

Let's repeat that creation process for the French version of the article.

- Title: **Blog article 1 (fr)**
- Content: This text is taken from http://lipsum.com. We used the second paragraph of their dummy text so that it looks different from the English content.

- Category: **Blog (fr) (fr-FR)**

- Language: **French (FR)**

- Click on the "Save" button to confirm our changes without leaving the screen:

- Click on the "Associations" tab so we can link the French version of the article to the English version:

- Click "Save & Close" to confirm our changes:

There we go. The two articles that we just created are linked together.

Let's do the whole process of creating the articles and associate them together one more time. When we do that, we will have two blog articles in each category of our blog, and they will be linked (associated) together, which clearly can be seen in the Article manager of the Joomla admin area.

Using the instructions provided earlier in this chapter, see if you can create a second English and French blog post. Your Articles screen will look like this:

⇕	☐	Status	Title	Access	Association	Author	Language
	☐	✔ ☆ ▼	Blog article 2 (fr) (Alias: blog-article-2 -fr) Category: Blog (fr)	Public	EN FR	Super User	▋▋French (FR)
	☐	✔ ☆ ▼	Blog article 2 (Alias as: blog-article-2) Category: Blog (en)	Public	EN FR	Super User	🇬🇧 English (en-GB)
	☐	✔ ☆ ▼	Blog article 1 (fr) (Alias: blog-article-1 -fr) Category: Blog (fr)	Public	EN FR	Super User	▋▋French (FR)
	☐	✔ ☆ ▼	Blog article 1 (Alias as: blog-article-1) Category: Blog (en)	Public	EN FR	Super User	🇬🇧 English (en-GB)

CREATING MULTILINGUAL JOOMLA MENUS

The next step in our process is to make the blog posts visible on the front end of our site.

We are going to make a link so the people can see either the multiple English articles in their category, or they can see the multiple French articles in their respective category.

By now, our process should start to feel familiar:

- We'll make an English menu link.

- We'll make a French menu link.

- We'll associate the two menu links together.

Let's see how that process works on our site:

- Go to "Menus", "Main menu (en-GB)" and then click on "Add New Menu Item":

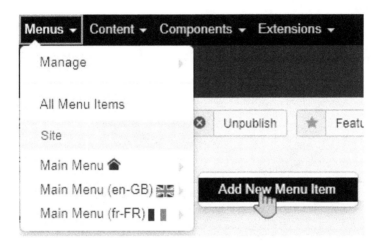

- Menu Title: **Blog (en)**

- Menu Item Type: Choose "Articles" and then "Category Blog":

Menu Item Type

- Language: **English (en-GB)**

- For the category, we'll choose the "Blog (en)" category that we created earlier in this chapter:

Select or Change Category

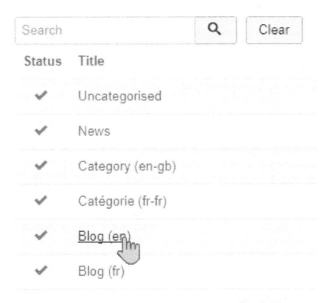

- When we have done that, click on "Save & Close":

- In the "Menu Items" manager, you should be able to see the new menu item that we have just created:

- Let us switch to the French menu. Choose "Main menu (fr-FR)" using the menu selection drop-down box:

- Click on "New":

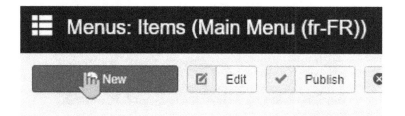

- Menu Title: **Blog (fr)**

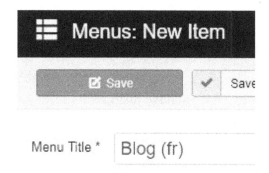

- Set the Menu Item Type to "Category blog", as we did for the English menu item:

- For category, we'll choose "Blog (fr)":

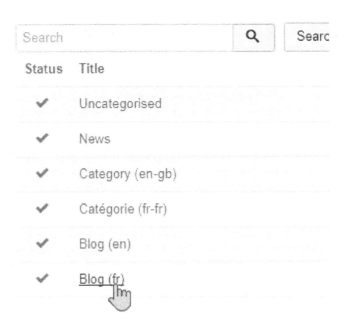

- On the right-hand side, choose "French" as the language for this menu item:

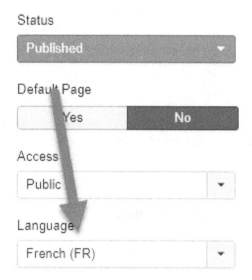

- Click "Save" to confirm our changes:

- Now we can associate the menu item with its English counterpart. Click on the "Associations" tab, and you should be able to choose the English menu item by clicking on the "Select" button:

- Click on the "Save & Close" button:

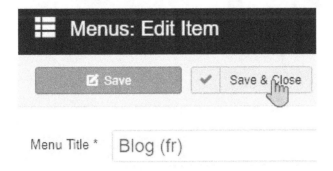

- We can now check if our work is effective on the front end of our site. Reload the home page of the site, and you should see the newly created menu item called "Blog (en)" that appears in the main menu.

- Click on "Blog (en)", and you will see our articles that we created earlier in the process.

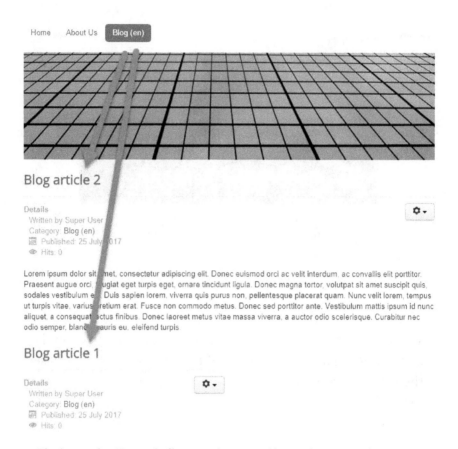

- Click on the French flag, and you will see the French menu with "Blog (fr)" included:

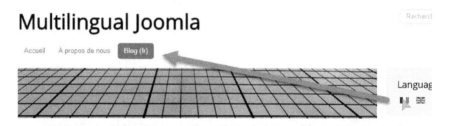

- You will also see the articles in French that we created earlier:

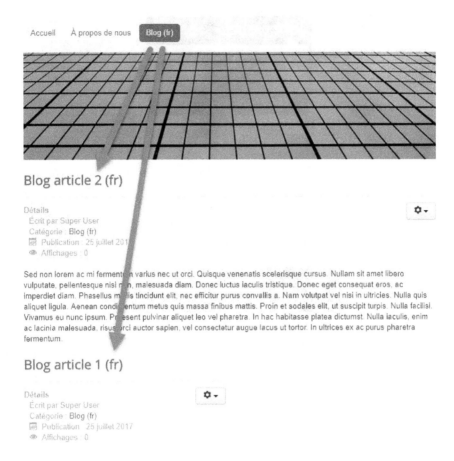

CREATING MULTILINGUAL JOOMLA MODULES

Now, let's complete the process of translating these categories, articles and menu links by placing a module on the right-hand side of our site. We are going to make a module which showcases the latest articles in both the English and the French category.

- Go back to the Joomla admin area.

- Go to "Extensions" and then "Modules":

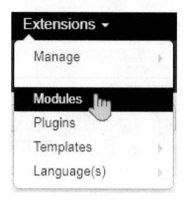

- By default, there isn't any kind of Latest Articles module. Let's click on "New" to create the module:

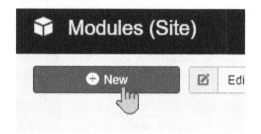

- Choose "Articles – Latest":

Select a Module Type:

Articles - Archived This module shows a list of the c

Articles - Categories This module displays a list of c

Articles - Category This module displays a list of art

Articles - Latest This module shows a list of the mos

Articles - Most Read This module shows a list of the

- Set the title of this module to "Blog Posts":

- Instead of showing "All categories", select only the **Blog (en) (en-GB)** category:

- On the right-hand side, set the language to **English (en-GB)**:

- Choose the position for the module: "position-7" works well for the default Joomla template:

- Click on the "Save & Close" button:

Repeat that process and create one more module to show the blog posts from the "Blog (fr)" category.

- Click on "New".
- Select "Article – Latest".
- Set the title of the module to **Publications du blog**:

Title * Publications du blog

- Choose **Blog (fr) (fr-FR):**

Articles - Latest

This module shows a li____ of the most recently published and current Arti____ though they are the most ____cent.

Category   Blog (fr) (fr-FR) ⊗

- Set the language of the module to **French (FR):**

Access

Public ▾

Ordering

1. News F___sh ▾

Language

French (FR) ▾

- Choose the position of the module and set it to the "position-7":

- Click on the "Save" button.
- You will notice with modules that there isn't actually an Association tab. You can associate categories, articles, menu links and many other things, but modules are an exception. Fortunately, this should still work effectively. Let's take a look.

- Go to the front of your site. On the right-hand side of the site, you will see our new module with the list of only the English blog posts:

- If you click on the French flag, you will see that the title and the content of our module have updated to be in French:

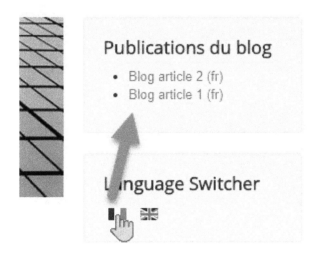

Congratulations! You have set up a complete blog in Joomla, using categories, articles, menus and modules.

What you have seen in this chapter is the big picture process of building a multilingual Joomla blog:

1. Create the categories, and associate them.
2. Create the articles, and associate them.
3. Create the menu links, and associate them.
4. Create the modules.

WHAT'S NEXT?

Now that you know how to translate Joomla content, we're going to move on to extensions.

Over the next few chapters, we'll show you how to translate the core Joomla extensions, plus any non-core extensions you want to use.

CHAPTER 8.

TRANSLATING A JOOMLA CONTACT FORM

We are making progress with our multilingual Joomla site and have a good idea of how to handle content on our site. Now let's take a look at how we can handle extensions.

In this chapter, we are going to show you how to create a contact form that is available in both English and French. The process is going to be very similar to the one that we used in previous chapters. Here's the process we're going to use:

1. Organize categories for the contact forms.
2. Create the contact forms, and associate them.
3. Create the menu links, and associate them.

MULTILINGUAL CONTACT FORM CATEGORIES

Let's see how that process works for contact forms:

- In the admin area of your site, go to "Components", and then to "Contacts":

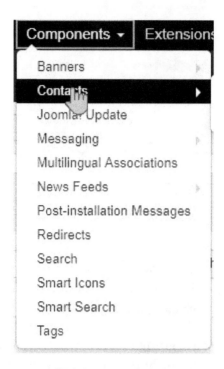

- Click the "Categories" link in the left-hand menu:

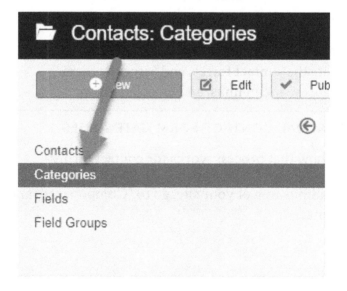

We do have a choice to make with categories:

- If we don't have a lot of contact forms, then we can leave it as

"Uncategorised" and put both English and French contacts in that category.

- If we have many contact forms, then it is probably best to create separate categories.

In this example, we're going to leave the default "Uncategorised" category alone and use it for all our contact forms. If you don't have an "Uncategorised" category, create it now.

MULTILINGUAL CONTACT FORMS

- Click "Contacts" in the left-hand menu:

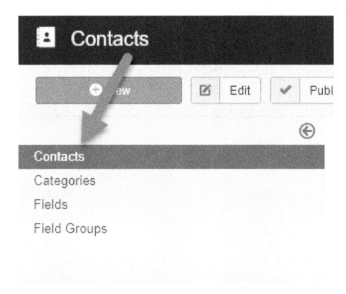

- Click on the title of the existing contact form:

- Enter your name in the Name field:

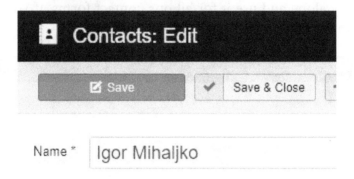

- Choose English (en-GB) for the Language option.
- Click on "Save & Close".

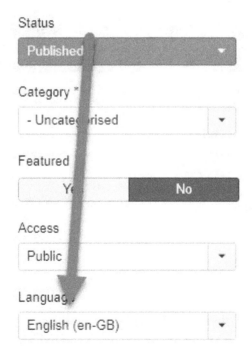

- Now, we have an English version of the contact form:

- Let's click the "New" button and create a French version of the contact form:

- Enter the French version of your name, if there is one. There is no special version of my name in French, so I will enter Igor Mihaljko again:

- Choose French (FR) for the Language option:

- Put your email address in the Email field:

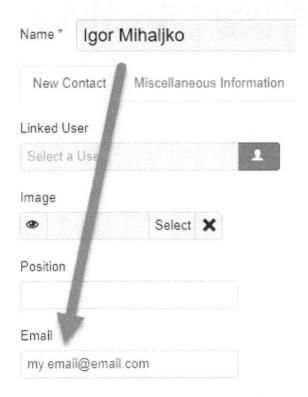

- Click on "Save" button to apply your changes:

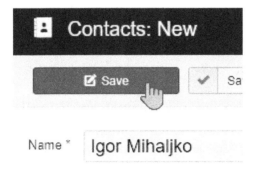

- After saving, click on the "Associations" tab:

- Click on the "Select" button and associate this French version of the contact form with the English version:

- Click on "Save & Close" to apply your changes.
- You will see that those two contact forms are now related:

MULTILINGUAL MENU LINKS TO CONTACT FORMS

- Go to "Menus", and then "Main Menu (en-GB)".
- Click on the "Add New Menu Item" link:

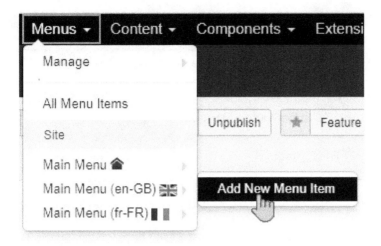

- Set the title of the menu item to "Contact Me":

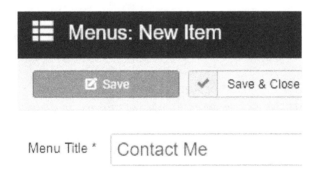

- Click on "Select" for the "Menu Item Type" option:

- Choose "Contacts" and then "Single Contact" item from the selection window:

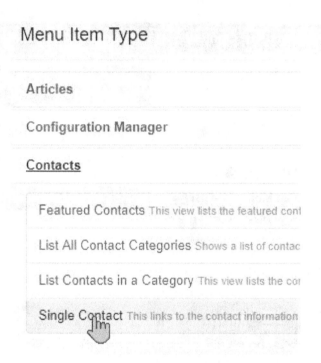

- Choose the English version of your contact form:

- Under the "Language" option, choose "English (en-GB)":

- Click on the "Save & Close" button to finish.

- In the "Main Menu (en-GB)", you can see the new menu item is linked to the English version of our Contact form:

		Status	Title	Menu	Home	Access	Association	Language	ID
⋮	☐	✔	Home (Alias: english-homepage) Articles » Featured Articles	Main Menu (en-GB)	🏴	Public	EN FR	🏴 English (en-GB)	117
⋮	☐	✔	About Us (Alias: about-us-en) Articles » Single Article	Main Menu (en-GB)	☆	Public	EN FR	🏴 English (en-GB)	119
⋮	☐	✔	Blog (en) (Alias: blog-en) Articles » Category Blog	Main Menu (en-GB)	☆	Public	EN FR	🏴 English (en-GB)	125
⋮	☐	✔	Contact Me (Alias: contact-me) Contacts » Single Contact	Main Menu (en-GB)	☆	Public		🏴 English (en-GB)	127

- Now let's go to the "Main Menu (fr-FR)":

- Click on the "New" button:

- For the "Menu Title", put in the French title "Contactez moi":

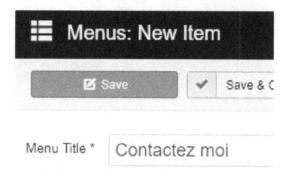

- For the menu item type, choose "Contacts" and then "Single Contact":

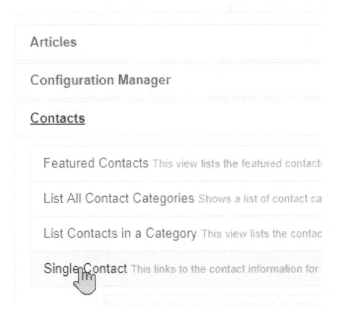

- Choose the French version of your contact form that you set up earlier:

- Under the "Language" option, choose "French (FR)":

- Click on the "Save" button.
- Click on the "Associations" tab.
- Click the "Select" button:

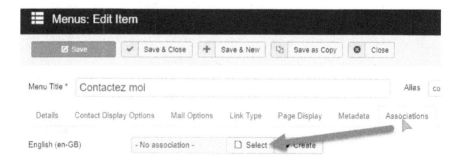

- Associate the French version of your menu item to the English version of the menu item:

- Click "Save & Close":

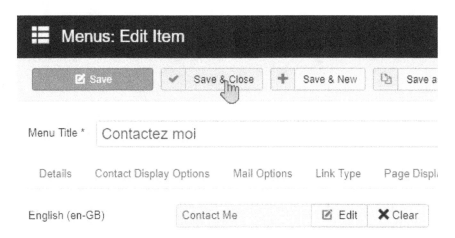

- Go to the front of your site. You will now have an English version of the "Contact Me" menu link:

- Click on the French flag and you will see the French version of the contact form. Since we uploaded the French language pack for Joomla, all of the default text is already translated into the French language.

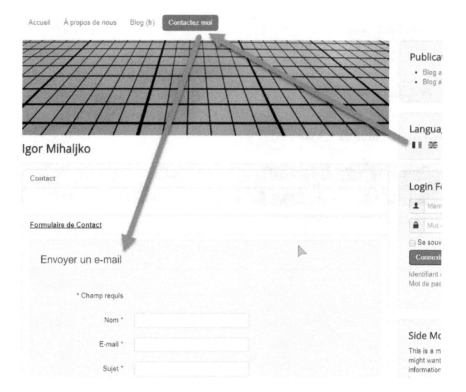

WHAT'S NEXT?

This same process will work for all of the default Joomla extensions. They will all have these multilingual capabilities.

Later on in this book, we are going to show you how to translate non-core extensions and templates.

In the next chapter, we are going to concentrate on cleaning up what we see in front of us. We are going to translate those last little items that haven't yet been fully translated into both English and French.

CHAPTER 9.

THE MULTILINGUAL ASSOCIATIONS COMPONENT

Throughout this book we've been relying on Associations to connect the different language versions of our site together.

We created those Associations one-by-one. We edited individual categories, articles, menu links and contact forms.

However, Joomla provides a component called Multilingual Associations, which gives you an overview of all the associations on your site. Multilingual Associations is available under the "Components" dropdown:

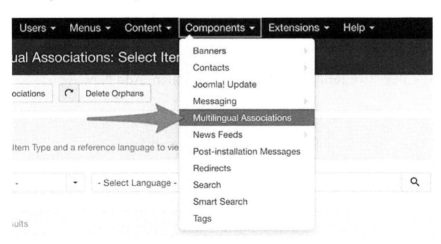

Inside the Multilingual Associations component you will be able to edit all your translations in a single interface. This will save you a lot of time and energy. This image below shows the current Multilingual Associations display for our site:

Let's see an example of how to use the Multilingual Associations component. Here's what we're going to do:

- We'll add a new English language article to the blog that we created in the chapter "Translating a Joomla Blog".

- We'll use the Multilingual Associations component to find the article that hasn't yet been translated.

- Inside the Multilingual Associations component, we'll open the English language article and translate the blog article into French.

Let's start that process and see how the Multilingual Associations component works:

- Click "Content", then "Articles", and then "Add New Article":

- Enter a title for the article. We've chosen "Blog article 3":

- Set the language of the article to English:

- Set the category of the article to "Blog (en)":

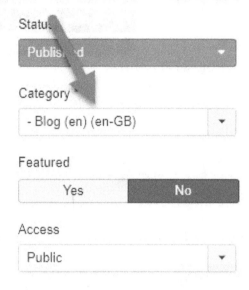

- Click on the "Save & Close" button.

Now that we have our new article ready, we can go to the Multilingual Associations component and search for the article we just saved, "Blog article 3":

- Go to "Components", and then "Multilingual Associations":

- From the "Select Item Type" dropdown, choose "Articles":

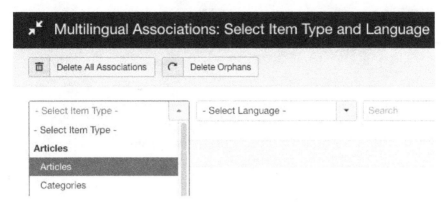

- From the "Select Langauge" dropdown, choose "English" (en-GB).

- You will see a list of articles in English:

- Click on the title of your newly created article:

- Your article will be loaded in the new page. The page is divided into two parts. The left side of the page represents the original article in English:

- On the right side of the page, choose French as your target language:

- You will now see that a new article area is available:

- Enter the details for the French blog post on the right side of the page:

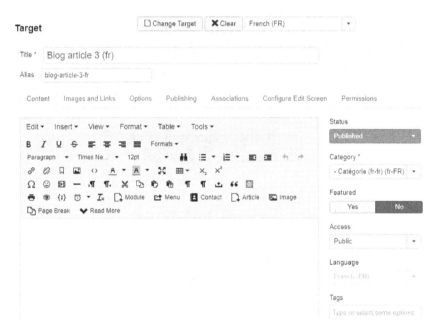

- If you do already have the target article created and ready, you can find the article by clicking on the "Select target" button:

- You can also copy over all the details from the original article by clicking on "Copy Reference to Target":

Notice that you can't change the language of the article. The "Language" option can't be selected. This is because we already chose French as our target language earlier in this process.

When you are satisfied with your new French article, notice that you have two Save options. You can click "Save Reference" to save the original article on the left of the screen:

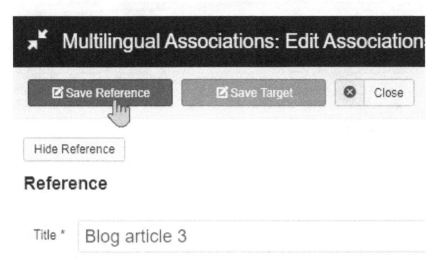

You can also click "Save Target" to save the target article on the right of the screen:

- Save both the target and reference articles.
- Go to the front end of the site to check that the English article is showing.

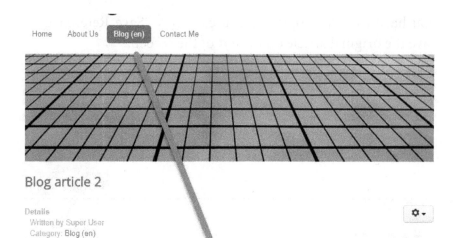

Blog article 2

Details
Written by Super User
Category: Blog (en)
🖼 Published: 25 July 2017
👁 Hits: 0

Lorem ipsum dolor sit amet, consectetur adipiscing elit. Donec euismod orci ac velit interdum, ac convallis elit porttitor. Praesent augue orci, feugiat eget turpis eget, ornare tincidunt ligula. Donec magna tortor, volutpat sit amet suscipit quis, sodales vestibulum elit. Duis sapien lorem, viverra quis purus non, pellentesque placerat quam. Nunc velit lorem, tempus ut turpis vitae, varius pretium erat. Fusce non commodo metus. Donec sed porttitor ante. Vestibulum mattis ipsum id nunc aliquet, a consequat lectus finibus. Donec laoreet metus vitae massa viverra, a auctor odio scelerisque. Curabitur nec odio semper, blandit mauris eu, eleifend turpis.

Blog article 1

Details
Written by Super User

Blog article 3

Details
Written by Super User

- If you browse the blog in French, you can see your new article there:

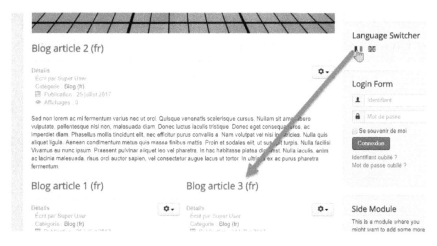

The last thing we want to point out in the Multilingual

Associations component is the "Not Associated" column. The "Not Associated" column allows you to find any areas of your site that still need translating:

Language	Associations	Not Associated
English (en-GB)		FR

I hope you agree that the Multilingual Associations component is a very useful new feature for building multilingual sites. The Multilingual Associations component can give you a better overview of the existing and missing associations in every area of your site.

WHAT'S NEXT?

The Multilingual Associations component allows you to translate many parts of your site, including articles, contact forms, menus, news feeds and more. Here's the dropdown from inside Multilingual Associations:

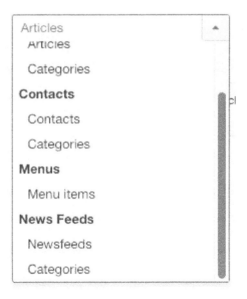

However, there are some items missing. Multilingual Associations does not cover modules, templates and some other smaller items on your site. In the next chapter, we're going to finish our site translation by focusing on those extra elements that we haven't translated yet.

CHAPTER 10.

COMPLETING THE SITE TRANSLATION

As you get close to finishing your multilingual Joomla site, it's time to take a look for items which haven't been translated.

If we examine the site, we are going to notice several things that haven't been fully translated.

For example, the title of the site is only available in English:

Multilingual Joomla

This module is also only available in English:

Side Module

This is a module where you might want to add some more information or an image, a link to your social media presence, or whatever makes sense for your site.

You can edit this module in the module manager. Look for the Side Module.

There are some smaller details as well. For example, the name of the "Login Form" module is still in English, even when the site is viewed in French:

In this chapter, we're going to show you how to think about tidying up those last few items. These text strings are going to be in some odd little corners of the site. You may have to dig around in order to translate these final items.

TRANSLATING THE SITE TITLE

First, let's translate the site title.

- In the admin area of the site, go to "Extensions" and then "Languages":

- Click "Content Languages":

- Click on the "French" link:

- Click on the "Site Name" tab:

- Enter a custom site name for the French site name:

Not every site will use this feature. For example, our company is called "OSTraining" in every language. However, it will be useful for some sites, and it is good to know that such possibility exists in the Joomla core.

- Save the language configuration and then go to the front of the site.
- Click on the French flag, and you will notice that the site title has been translated into the French site name you previously chose:

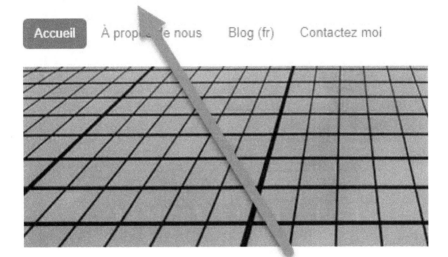

French site name

| **Accueil** | À prop... de nous | Blog (fr) | Contactez moi |

Article (fr-fr)

Détails

TRANSLATING MODULES

Next let's take a look at how to translate modules. For this example, we'll translate the Side Module. However, once you know these steps, you can apply the same steps to translate other modules as well.

- In the admin area of the site, go to "Extensions" and then "Modules".

- Look for "Side Module":

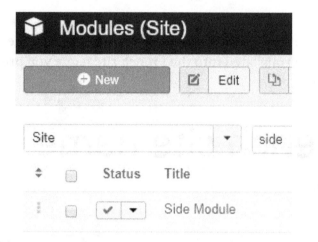

- Click on the "Side Module" title to edit it:

- From the module configuration screen, set the language of the module to English:

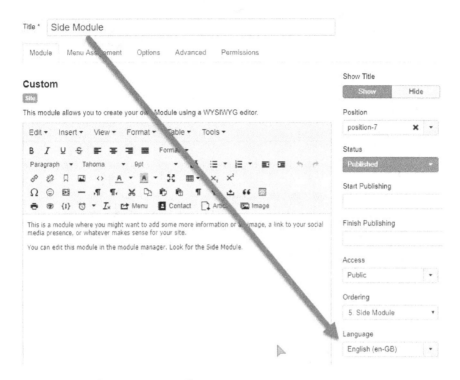

- Click on "Save as Copy":

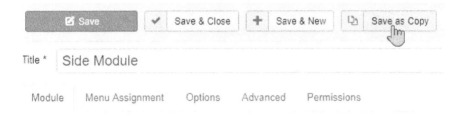

- Next, translate the title and text into French. To keep things simple, we've used Google Translate at https://translate.google.com to quickly translate the English text into some French:

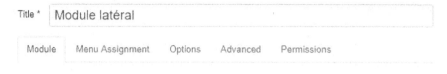

Custom

This module allows you to create your own Module using a WYSIWYG editor.

Il s'agit d'un module où vous voudrez peut-être ajouter plus d'informations ou une image, un lien vers la présence de vos médias sociaux ou tout ce qui est logique pour votre site.

Vous pouvez éditer ce module dans le gestionnaire de modules. Recherchez le module latéral.

- Set the status of the module to "Published":

- Set the language of the module to French:

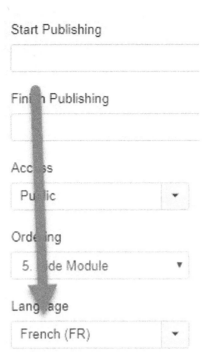

Start Publishing

Finish Publishing

Access

Public

Ordering

5. ide Module

Language

French (FR)

- Remember, there are no associations available with modules, so click on the "Save & Close" button to confirm the changes:

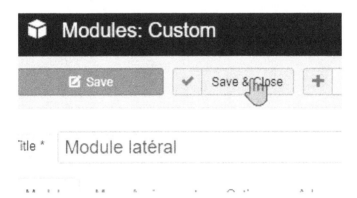

- Visit the front end of your site, and you'll notice that there is a French version of the module available:

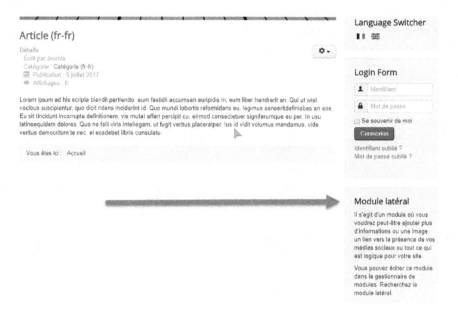

- Click on the English flag, and we now have the English version:

At this point, you may notice that the English and French modules are in a different order. If we want to make the site exactly the same, go back to "Extensions" and "Modules", then reorder the modules using drag-and-drop.

If you don't see the drag-and-drop option for modules, click the arrows in the "Ordering" column:

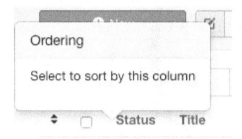

If I refresh the front end of the site, I should see that modules are now in the correct order:

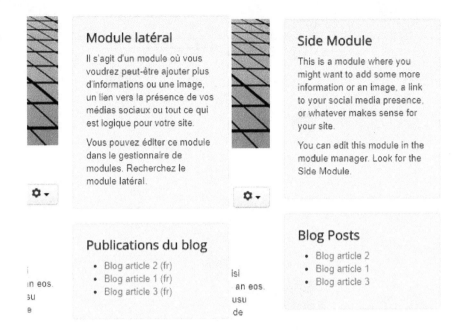

TRANSLATING THE LOGIN FORM MODULE

We still have an issue with the French version of the site. The "Login Form" module still has the title in English:

What we need to do is go to the Login Form module and configure it for the specific language.

- Go to "Extensions" then "Modules".
- Click on the title of the "Login Form" module:

- Set the Language of this module to English:

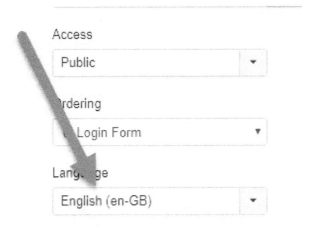

- Click on "Save as Copy":

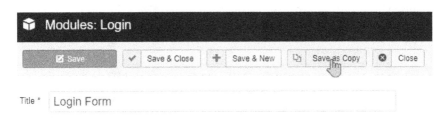

- Put the title of the login form in French. For example, let's put the title as "Formulaire de connexion":

- Set the module to be "Published":

- For the language of this module, choose French:

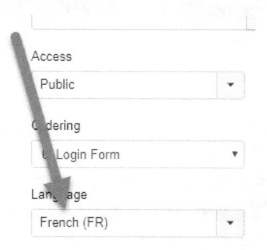

- Click on the "Save & Close" button:

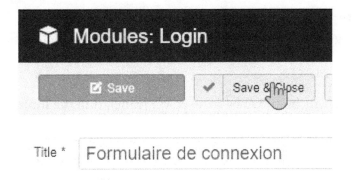

Title * Formulaire de connexion

- If you refresh the front end of the site, you should see the French version of the Login Form module:

Now, if we browse around the site using the non-default language, we should see that the entire site has been translated properly into French.

If there are any items that have not been translated, hopefully you have a good idea of how those final elements can be translated.

WHAT'S NEXT?

So far in this book we've focused on translating the Joomla core.

However, most sites are built using many non-core extensions. In the next two chapters, we'll show you how to translate extensions that aren't part of the Joomla core.

CHAPTER 11.

TRANSLATING NON-CORE EXTENSIONS

Up until this point, we have shown you how to translate the core of a Joomla site. We have translated articles, menus, modules, and default extensions.

In the next few chapters, we'll show you how to translate non-core extensions. In this chapter, we're going to focus on extensions that already have translations available. We're going to take you through the process of finding and installing translations for three Joomla extensions: ReReplacer, JEvents and Akeeba Backup.

It's worth noting that this may not be as smooth of an experience as it was when we were translating the Joomla core. This is because each developer decides whether or not to provide translations for their extension. Often these developers don't speak more than one language, and often they don't have a large team around them.

INSTALLING THE BACKEND LANGUAGE SWITCHER EXTENSION

Before we get into translating extensions, we need to know whether our extensions have been translated. We're going to install an extension that will make it much easier to test this.

As we've seen throughout this book, we use flags to easily click back-and-forth between languages when we are at the front end of our site. In the admin area of our site, there's no easy way to switch between languages to see if the translation has been successful.

To make this process easier, we're going to install an extension called Backend Language Switcher:

- Follow this link: https://joomla-extensions.kubik-rubik.de/bls-backend-language-switcher.

- Scroll down to the bottom of the page and click on the "BLS – Backend Language Switcher – Joomla! 3" link:

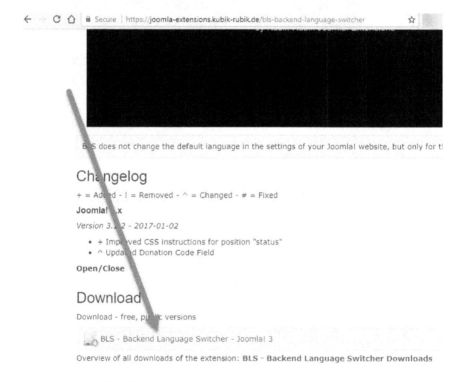

- Click on the checkbox for "I agree to the terms listed above".
- Click on the "Download" button:

The development and availability of the extension can be supported by purchasing a Donation Code. Once purchased and entered in the settings, the Donation Code must be validated and checked for authenticity through the project website. This checking request can only be performed when the code and the host are sent to the project website. This request is only performed if a Donation Code is entered! Additional Information: Donation Code System

☑ **I agree to the terms listed above -** Download

- The module will download to your computer.
- Go to "Extensions", "Manage" and then "Install":

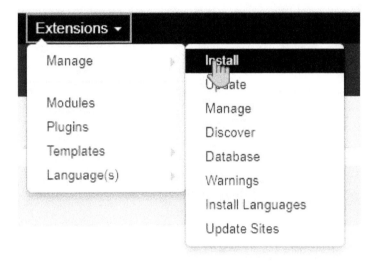

- Click on the "Upload Package File" tab.
- Drag-and-drop the module we just downloaded:

Upload & Install Joomla Extension

- After a few moments, you should see the "Installation of the module was successful" message:

Message
Installation of the module was successful.

BLS - Backend Language Switcher

This administration module can change the set language within seconds in the backend. The module creates a drop-down languages are listed. By clicking, the selected language is loaded and you can continue working on the same page. This is language files or if you want to create screenshots of different languages.

BLS does not change the default language in the settings of your Joomla! website, but only for the current session.

Next steps after the installation:

1. Select 'Extensions' - 'Modules'
2. Change the module type of 'Site' to 'Administrator' (at the left in the drop-down lists)
3. Choose 'BLS - Backend Language Switcher'
4. Set or enter the position 'menu' or 'status' and set the status to 'Published'

Project page: BLS - Backend Language Switcher

Please write a review in the JED: BLS - Backend Language Switcher in the Joomla! Extensions Directory - Thank you!

- Go to "Extensions", and then "Modules":

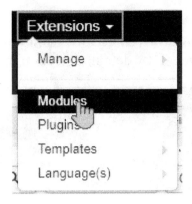

- In the site area drop-box, select "Administrator":

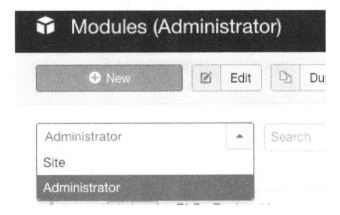

- In the list of modules, find "BLS – Backend Language Switcher". Click on the title of the module to edit it.

- Set the "position" option to "menu".

- Set the module to "Published":

- Look at the right top corner of your admin area, and you will notice a new item which shows the language that you are using at the moment. By default that should be "en-GB":

- If you click that item, you will see a drop down menu with all the installed languages listed:

- Click on the French language link, and your admin area language should switch to the French language:

This simple option will save us a lot of time as we test the extensions in this chapter.

USING THE TRANSLATION INCLUDED WITH AN EXTENSION

This first extension translation will be the easiest. We're going to translate an extension called ReReplacer, which allows you to temporarily replace text on your site. For example, if your company name changes, you can use ReReplacer to automatically update all uses of the old name.

- Go to the admin area of your Joomla site. Go to "Extensions", "Manage" and then click on the "Install" menu item:

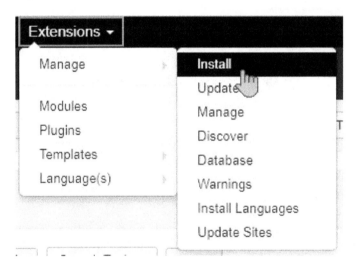

- Under the "Install from Web", we are going to search for an extension called ReReplacer:

rereplacer   🔍 ✕

Popular extensions listed on the Joomla Extension Directory

143 reviews with a
score of 100/100

ReReplacer

ReReplacer - search
and replace in your
websites output.
ReReplacer is a
Joomla! component
and system plugin that
enables you to replace
anything in your

- Go through the installation process for ReReplacer:

ReReplacer

143 reviews with a score of 100/100

Version: 8.1.0 (last update on Thursday, 27 July 2017)

License: GPLv2 or later   Free download

Added On: Wednesday, 12 March 2008

Component Plugin

✔ Install...   ▤ Directory Listing   ↪ Developer Website

- After the installation is complete, you'll see this "Regular Labs – ReReplacer" link in the "Components" menu:

- Inside ReReplacer, click "New".
- The whole interface of ReReplacer is running in English:

- In the top-right corner of the site, switch from English to French.

- You will notice that almost the entire extension is now running in French:

That's it. Sometimes it's really that easy. Some extensions, such as ReReplacer come with their own default language files. You don't need to do anything.

INSTALLING A NEW LANGUAGE FILE

Some developers ask you to go to their website to download translation files. Let's see an example of that process with JEvents, a popular calendar extension.

- Go to the admin area of your site. Click "Extensions", then "Manage" and finally "Install":

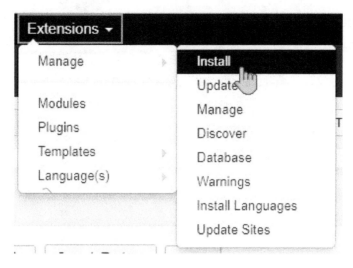

- Click the "Install from Web" tab.
- Search for JEvents in the search box:

- Click on the JEvents search result and complete the installation process:

JEvents

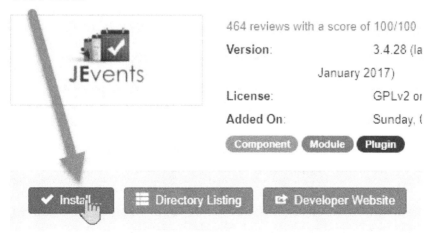

- After the installation, you'll see a screen like this:

- Go to "Components", and you will see a new menu item for JEvents:

- Clicking on the JEvents link leads us to the extension configuration in English:

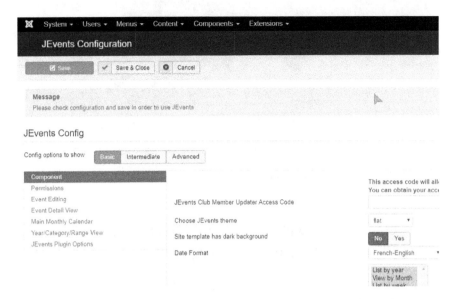

The next step is more tricky. We need to actually find a French language translation of JEvents. To be honest, in most cases the easiest thing to do is to do a Google search to see if you can find a translation.

- Go to the Google and type "jevents french translation" into the search box:

- The very first link in the search results is the one we are looking for:

- Clicking that link will take us to the direct JEvents French language translation file download page:

- Click to download the language translation files:

French language for JEvents

Download fr-FR_JEvents.zip

- Go back to your Joomla admin area.

We're going to install the downloaded file in the same way we would install a normal Joomla extension. Technically, Joomla treats a language pack as if it were an extension.

- Click on "Extensions", then "Manage" and finally on the "Install" link:

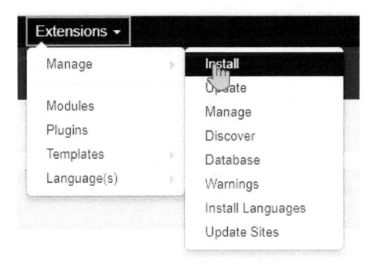

- Click on the "Upload Package File" tab.
- The easiest way to install the package that we just downloaded is to drag it into the area that says "Drag and drop file here to upload". Drop the French language package onto the designated area, and the installation process will automatically start.

Install from Web   Upload Package File   Install from Folder   Install from URL

Upload & Install Joomla Extension

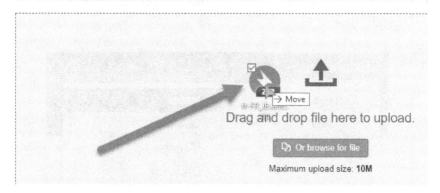

- After a few seconds, you will see a message saying that the installation of the file was successful:

French Language for JEvents

The easiest way to test the translation of the jEvents in the French language is to use the Backend Language Switcher.

- Click on the French language link, and your admin area language will switch to the French language.

- Go to "Components", and then click on the "JEvents menu item":

- You should see that the JEvents component area has been translated into French:

What about the front end of the site? Will our site visitors be able to view JEvents translated into both English and French?

- Use the Backend Language Switcher to move the admin area back to English.

That being done, I am going to make an English link and a French link from my Menus.

- Go to "Menus", and then "Main Menu (en-GB)".
- Click on the "Add New Menu Item" link.

- Call this new menu item "Events":

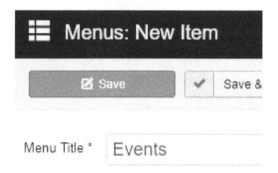

- Click "Select" for "Menu item type":

- From the list of menu item types, choose "JEvents – Core" and then "Date range":

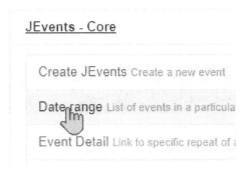

- On the right-hand side, set the language to English:

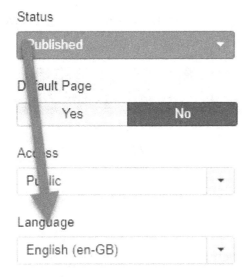

- Click on the "Save & Close" button:

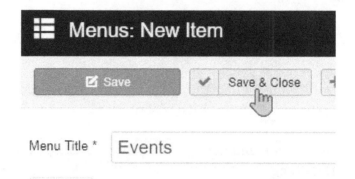

- Go to "Main Menu (fr-FR)" and repeat the process. Click on "New":

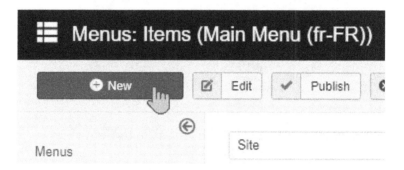

- Enter a French title for the menu item, which would be "Événements":

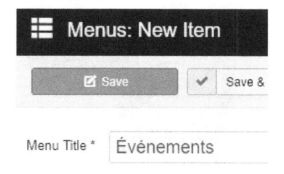

- Choose the menu item type. From the list of menu item types, choose "JEvents – Core" and then "Date range"

- On the right-hand side, set the language to French:

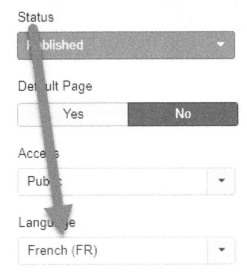

- Click on the "Save" button:

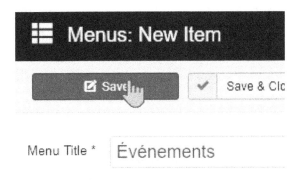

- Choose the "Associations" tab.
- Link your two new menu items together:

- Click on the "Save & Close" button:

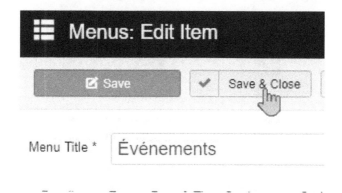

- Visit the front end of the site to see if it is working successfully. You will see a new link called "Events":

- On the "Events" screen, you'll see everything is successfully working in English, even if we don't have any events listed so far:

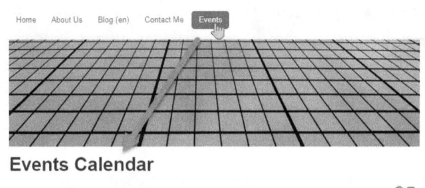

Events Calendar

By Year	By Month	By Week	Today	Jump to month

18 July 2017 - 25 August 2017

No events were found

- Click on the French flag, and you'll see the French version is also working. We have a calendar that is successfully set up in French.

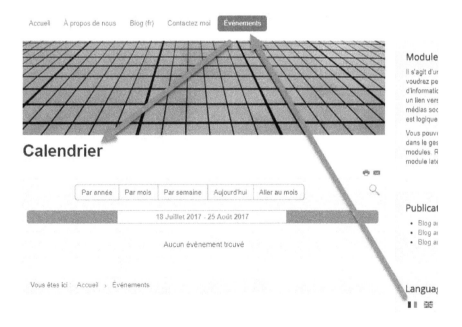

Let's try to install and translate another extension. This time we are going to try Akeeba Backup, which is a popular way of making backup copies of your Joomla website.

- Go to the admin area of the site, and click "Extensions", "Manage" and then "Install":

- Under the "Install from Web" tab, Akeeba Backup should be one of the first and most popular of all the extensions available:

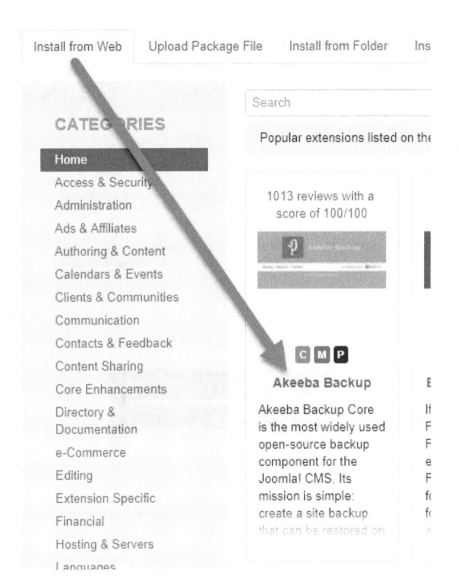

- Click on the Akeeba Backup item and complete the installation process:

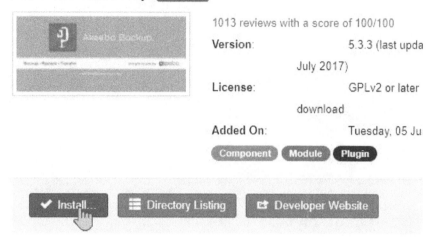

- Go to "Components", and then "Akeeba Backup":

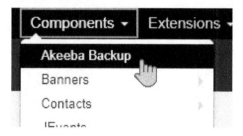

- Akeeba Backup has a Configuration wizard to go through in order to set up your site correctly:

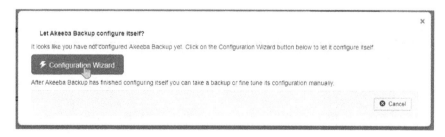

- When the process is finished, click on the "Configuration" button:

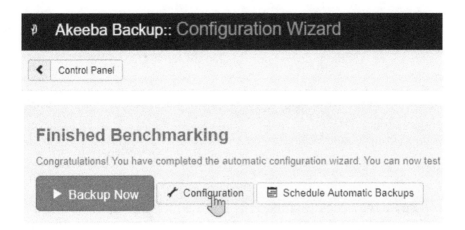

- You will be taken to the Akeeba Backup configuration screen. Everything is in English and seems to be working correctly:

Now that we have everything in English, we need to translate this into the French.

Again, we'll use Google to see if we can find the translation in French. Let's search for "Akeeba backup translation":

Google | Akeeba backup translation

All | Videos | Images | News | More

About 400 results (0.55 seconds)

Akeeba Backup Translations
https://cdn.akeebabackup.com/language/akeebabackup/index.html ▾
Feb 19, 2017 - These packages will only install the translation files on your site
the component itself. Please download the component ...

- They have a big download list from which I am going to find
  the French language file and download it to my computer:

Akeeba Backup Language Files

This page was last updated on 19 Feb 2017 09:42:41 GMT

WARNING! These packages will only install the translation files on your site. The

Not all languages are fully translated. Please check out the current translation

	af-ZA	Afrikaans (South Africa)	Download for Joomla! 3.x
	ar-AA	Arabic	Download for Joomla! 3.x
	az-AZ	Azeri (Azerbaijan)	Download for Joomla! 3.x
	bg-BG	Bulgarian (Bulgaria)	Download for Joomla! 3.x
	ca-ES	Catalan (Spain)	Download for Joomla! 3.x
	cs-CZ	Czech (Czech Republic)	Download for Joomla! 3.x
	da-DK	Danish (Denmark)	Download for Joomla! 3.x
	de-DE	German (Germany)	Download for Joomla! 3.x
	el-GR	Greek (Greece)	Download for Joomla! 3.x
	en-GB	English (United Kingdom)	Download for Joomla! 3.x
	es-ES	Spanish (Spain)	Download for Joomla! 3.x
	et-EE	Estonian (Estonia)	Download for Joomla! 3.x
	fa-IR	Farsi (Iran)	Download for Joomla! 3.x
	fi-FI	Finnish (Finland)	Download for Joomla! 3.x
	fr-FR	French (France)	Download for Joomla! 3.x
	hr-HR	Croatian (Croatia)	Download for Joomla! 3.x
	hu-HU	Hungarian (Hungary)	Download for Joomla! 3.x

- Go to the admin area of your site again. Go to "Extensions", "Manage" and then "Install":

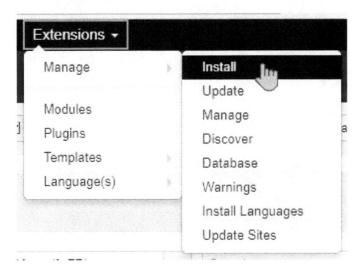

- Click the "Upload Package File" tab and drag and drop the language package that we have just downloaded:

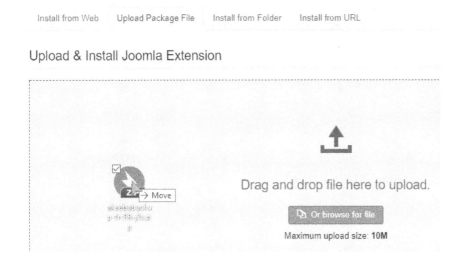

- After a few moments, you will see a message that says that the package was installed successfully.

Message

Installation of the file was successful.

French (France) translation file for Akeeba Backup

- As before, the best way to test this is to switch the language of the admin area to French using the language switcher:

- When the admin area has been switched to French, click on "Components" and then on "Akeeba Backup":

- You will now see that Akeeba Backup is successfully translated into French:

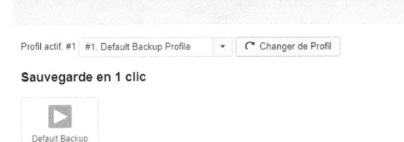

Profil actif: #1 | #1. Default Backup Profile ▼ | C Changer de Profil

Sauvegarde en 1 clic

WHAT'S NEXT?

In this chapter, we worked with three extensions where translations were already available.

In the next chapter, we are going to talk about what to do if you can't find a translation for an extension that you really want to use.

CHAPTER 12.

TRANSLATING NON-CORE EXTENSIONS MANUALLY

So far in this book, we have shown you how to translate the Joomla core and extensions that come with a translation already provided for you.

However, you may find yourself in a situation where a translation is just not available for the extension that you want to use.

In this chapter, we're going to show you how to translate an extension that does not have a translation.

SETTING UP OSDOWNLOADS IN ENGLISH AND FRENCH

- Go to the admin area of your Joomla site. Go to "Extensions", "Manage" and then click on the "Install" menu item.

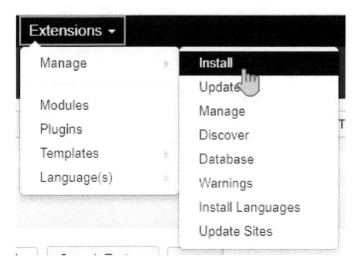

- Under the "Install from Web", we are going to search for an extension called OSDownloads, which is a really quick and easy way to provide file downloads for your users.

- Click on the "OSDownloads" item in the search result panel:

osdownloads

Popular extensions listed on the Joomla Extensior

17 reviews with a
score of 100/100

OSDownloads

C M

OSDownloads

OSDownloads is the easiest way to add
downloads to Joomla. OSDownloads
gives you an easy and reliable
downloads directory. OSDownloads also
integrates directly to MailChimp and
Constant Contact so you can collect
emails in exchange for downloads. You
can use OSDownloads to build your

- Click on the "Install" button:

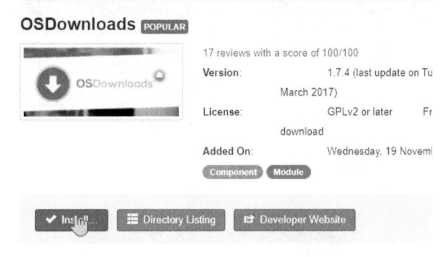

- Click on the next "Install" button also:

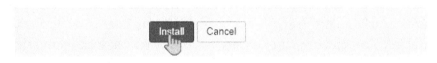

- After a few moments, you should see a message that says that the installation was successful.

OSDownloads is an extension to help you manage your downloads. It allows you to easily |

- If you go to "Components" and the "OSDownloads Free", you should see that everything is set up and everything is in English:

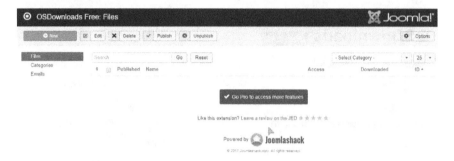

- Switch the backend language to French using the switcher module from the previous chapter:

You may not see many changes at all. There are some buttons that are translated to French, but those buttons are using Joomla's default French language strings. All the other page elements that are using OSDownloads string constants are not translated into the French language.

Let us show you what to do if you find yourself in a similar situation and don't have a translation available for the extension that you want to use.

- First, switch back from French to English:

Next, we're going to repeat the same process that we did earlier in the book. We're going to make an English language menu link and a French language menu link.

- Go to "Menus", and then to "Main Menu (en-GB)". Click on the "Add New Menu Item" link:

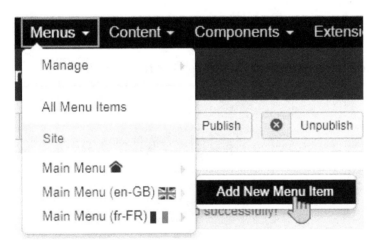

- Set the "Menu Title" to "Downloads":

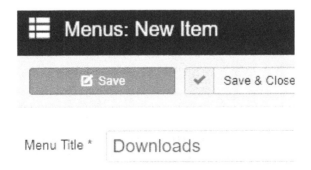

- The menu item type will be "OSDownloads Free" and then "Category File List":

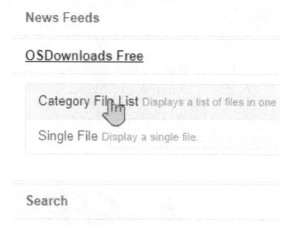

- Choose English as the language for this menu item:

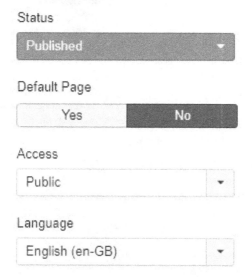

- OSDownloads has one required option for the menu link: Categories. We are going to choose "General", which is the default category for the extension:

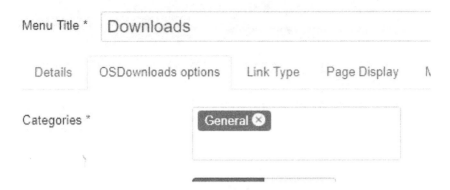

- Click on the "Save & Close" button:

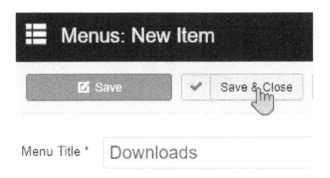

- Now, we need to make a French language menu link. Choose "Main Menu (fr-FR)":

- Repeat the same process we used for the English menu link to create the French menu item. Click "New":

- Make a French version of our Downloads link. Let's call this "Téléchargements":

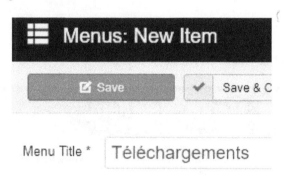

- The menu item type will be "OSDownloads Free" and then "Category File List" again:

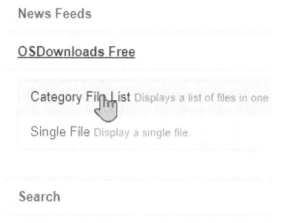

- On the right-hand side, choose French as the language for this menu item:

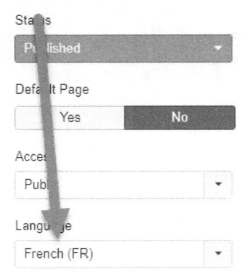

- In the "OSDownloads options" tab, choose the "General" category:

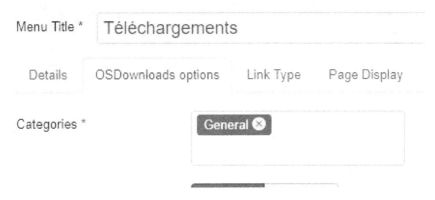

- Click "Save".
- On the Associations tab, link those two menu items together:

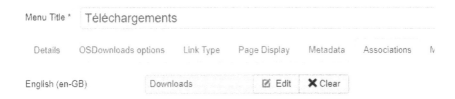

- Click "Save & Close":

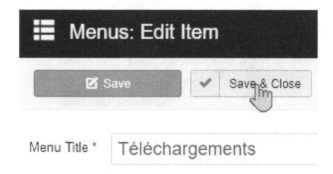

What we're going to do next is a little bit of a workaround because we know that OSDownloads is not translated into the French language.

- Go to "Components", then "OSDownloads Free", and then "Categories":

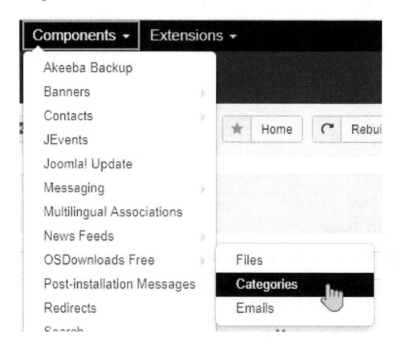

We need to create a category for our English downloads and a category for our French downloads as well. Since we have the

General category already set up, it's easiest to just rename this for our English downloads.

- Click on the "General" category.
- Change the name to "English downloads":

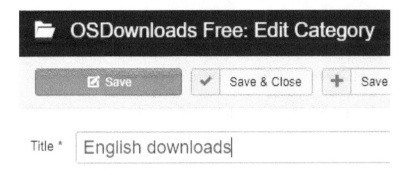

- Click on the "Save & New" button.
- Let's et up another category specifically for our French downloads:

- Click on "Save & Close":

Now we have two categories for our two languages.

- Click on the "Files" link on the left-hand side.

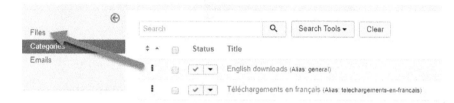

- Click on "New".
- Enter "English File" for the Name:

- Choose a file to upload. You can select any file from your computer:

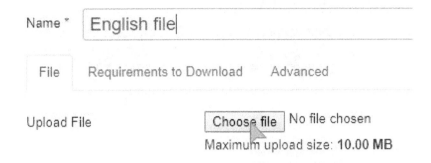

- Click "Save & Close":

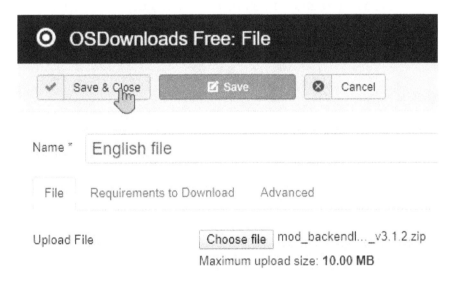

- Repeat the process and create a French version of the file as well. Click on "New" again:

- Name this file "Fichier français":

- Choose a file to upload. Again, almost any file will work from your computer:

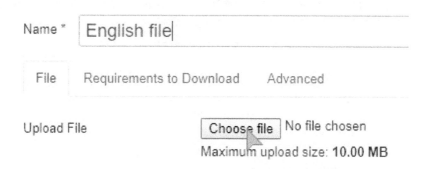

- Choose the French category that you created:

- Click on "Save & Close" again to confirm the changes:

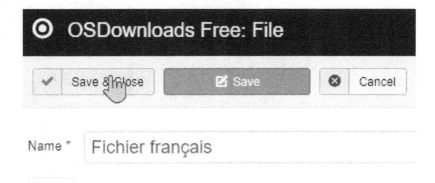

- Congratulations! Now you have an English file in the Downloads category and a French file in the French version of the downloads category:

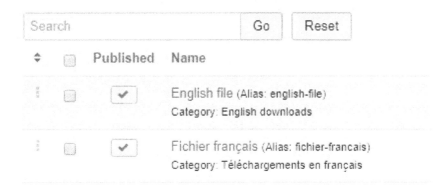

There is only one more thing to do, and that is to update our menu link to actually point to the French category.

- Go to Menus, and then to "Main Menu (fr-FR)":

- Open up the download link in French:

- Make sure that it points to the downloads category in the French language:

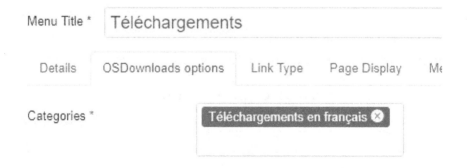

- Click on "Save & Close":

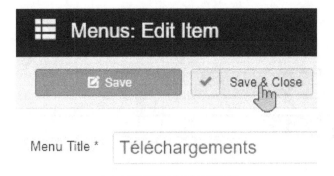

Menu Title * Téléchargements

- Now, go to the front end of your site. Click on the "Downloads" menu item:

- We can see the English downloads category and the English file available for the download:

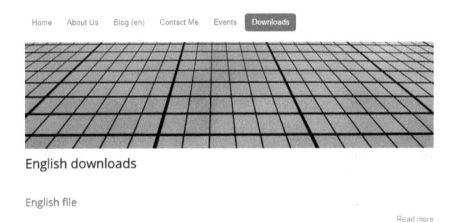

English downloads

English file

Read more

- Change your site to the French language, and it seems to be translated successfully. We have the category in French, and we have our file available in French as well:

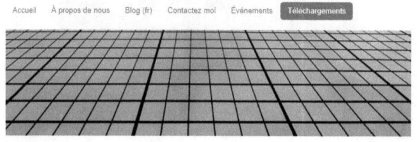

Téléchargements en français

Fichier français

- However, there is one exception down on the right-hand side of the downloads. We still see the text of the "Read more" link in English.

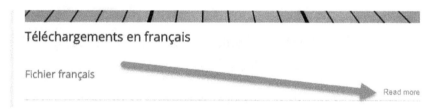

Téléchargements en français

Fichier français   Read more

In order to fix this, we need to dig down into the file system in order to make the translation successful.

TRANSLATING OSDOWNLOADS VIA THE FILE SYSTEM

In order to translate the "Read more" text string, we need to dig down into the file system of our site. We're looking at the files from our multilingual site:

Name	Size	Changed	Rights	Owner
..		5.7.2017. 7:55:55	rwxr-x---	
administrator		4.7.2017. 9:04:12	rwxr-xr-x	
bin		4.7.2017. 9:04:12	rwxr-xr-x	
cache		4.7.2017. 9:04:12	rwxr-xr-x	
cli		4.7.2017. 9:04:12	rwxr-xr-x	
components		25.7.2017. 14:32:13	rwxr-xr-x	
images		5.7.2017. 9:49:28	rwxr-xr-x	
includes		4.7.2017. 9:04:12	rwxr-xr-x	
language		14.7.2017. 14:30:33	rwxr-xr-x	
layouts		4.7.2017. 9:04:12	rwxr-xr-x	
libraries		25.7.2017. 14:08:17	rwxr-xr-x	
media		25.7.2017. 14:32:13	rwxr-xr-x	
modules		25.7.2017. 14:32:14	rwxr-xr-x	
plugins		4.7.2017. 9:04:12	rwxr-xr-x	
templates		4.7.2017. 9:04:12	rwxr-xr-x	
tmp		25.7.2017. 14:32:14	rwxr-xr-x	
.htaccess	3 KB	5.7.2017. 9:34:20	rw-r--r--	
configuration.php	4 KB	5.7.2017. 9:34:50	r--r--r--	
index.php	2 KB	4.7.2017. 9:04:12	rw-r--r--	
Joomla_3.7.3-Stable-Full_Package.zip	12.734 KB	4.7.2017. 14:28:51	rw-r--r--	
LICENSE.txt	18 KB	4.7.2017. 9:04:12	rw-r--r--	
README.txt	5 KB	4.7.2017. 9:04:12	rw-r--r--	

We see the main folders of the Joomla system, including "administrator", "components", "images". We can also see a "language" folder there too:

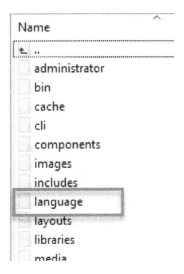

- Open that folder and inside we see "en-GB" and "fr-FR" folders:

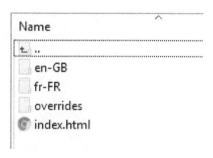

- The files inside this folder contain many of the language strings for our site. If we click on the "en-GB" folder, there is a good chance that we are going to find a file specifically for OSDownloads:

Name	Size	Changed
↵ ..		14.7.2017. 14:30:3:
en-GB.com_ajax.ini	1 KB	4.7.2017. 9:04:12
en-GB.com_akeeba.ini	1 KB	25.7.2017. 14:08:1{
en-GB.com_config.ini	3 KB	4.7.2017. 9:04:12
en-GB.com_contact.ini	4 KB	4.7.2017. 9:04:12
en-GB.com_content.ini	6 KB	4.7.2017. 9:04:12
en-GB.com_finder.ini	4 KB	4.7.2017. 9:04:12
en-GB.com_jevents.ini	17 KB	25.7.2017. 13:40:5{
en-GB.com_mailto.ini	1 KB	4.7.2017. 9:04:12
en-GB.com_media.ini	5 KB	4.7.2017. 9:04:12
en-GB.com_messages.ini	1 KB	4.7.2017. 9:04:12
en-GB.com_newsfeeds.ini	2 KB	4.7.2017. 9:04:12
en-GB.com_osdownloads.ini	2 KB	25.7.2017. 14:32:1:
en-GB.com_osdownloads.sys.ini	1 KB	25.7.2017. 14:32:1:
en-GB.com_search.ini	2 KB	4.7.2017. 9:04:12

- There is going to be a separate file for each component and each module. The file called "en-GB.com_osdownloads.ini" is the one we want to find:

Name	Size	Changed
⬏ ..		14.7.2017. 14:30:3:
en-GB.com_ajax.ini	1 KB	4.7.2017. 9:04:12
en-GB.com_akeeba.ini	1 KB	25.7.2017. 14:08:1{
en-GB.com_config.ini	3 KB	4.7.2017. 9:04:12
en-GB.com_contact.ini	4 KB	4.7.2017. 9:04:12
en-GB.com_content.ini	6 KB	4.7.2017. 9:04:12
en-GB.com_finder.ini	4 KB	4.7.2017. 9:04:12
en-GB.com_jevents.ini	17 KB	25.7.2017. 13:40:5{
en-GB.com_mailto.ini	1 KB	4.7.2017. 9:04:12
en-GB.com_media.ini	5 KB	4.7.2017. 9:04:12
en-GB.com_messages.ini	1 KB	4.7.2017. 9:04:12
en-GB.com_newsfeeds.ini	2 KB	4.7.2017. 9:04:12
en-GB.com_osdownloads.ini	2 KB	25.7.2017. 14:32:1:
en-GB.com_osdownloads.sys.ini	1 KB	25.7.2017. 14:32:1:
en-GB.com_search.ini	2 KB	4.7.2017. 9:04:12

- Inside that file, we are going to find all of the different language strings for this extension. If we open it up, this is what we should see:

- Inside the file we can see the "Read more" text that we to want to change.

```
25
26    COM_OSDOWNLOADS_NO_DOWNLOADS="There are no downloads to disp
27    COM_OSDOWNLOADS_READ_MORE ="Read more"
28
```

There are also all the other language strings that the OSDownloads extension is using. So this is the file that we want if we want to change the language in OSDownloads.

- Download the file to your local computer:

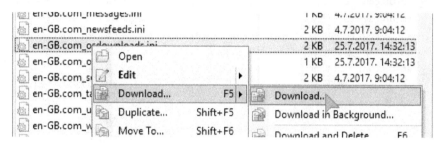

- Leave the "en-BG" folder.
- Go into the "fr-FR" folder.
- Upload your downloaded file into the French folder:

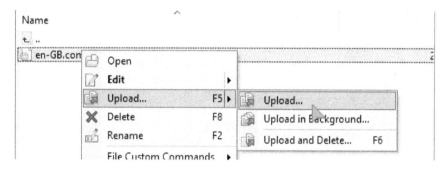

- The file that we uploaded has the wrong name for the French language file. We're going to rename the file to "fr-FR.com_osdownloads.ini":

- Now we have a French version of the language file for the OSDownloads component. However, it is still full of the

English language strings. We need to open that file now and translate the "Read more" text into French:

```
25
26      COM_OSDOWNLOADS_NO_DOWNLOADS="There are no downloads to display."
27      COM_OSDOWNLOADS_READ_MORE ="Lire la suite"
28
29      COM_OSDOWNLOADS_SUPPORT ="Support"
30
```

- Save the translations in your new file.

- Go to the front end of your site. You will see that my French download section is now completely translated into French:

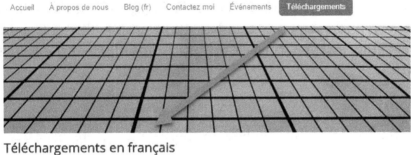

Téléchargements en français

A quick note of caution. Everything that you see in the language folder is for the front end of the site. There is a second language folder for the admin area of the site. If you go to the "administrator" folder there is going to be a "language" folder there as well.

Name		Size	Changed
⌐ ..			5.7.2017. 9:34:20
cache			4.7.2017. 9:04:12
components			25.7.2017. 14:32:13
help			4.7.2017. 9:04:12
includes			4.7.2017. 9:04:12
language			14.7.2017. 14:30:33
logs			4.7.2017. 9:04:12
manifests			4.7.2017. 9:04:12
modules			5.7.2017. 9:49:28

/multilingual/administrator/

If you open up the "language" folder inside the "administrator" folder, you are going to see "en-GB" and "fr-FR" folders again. If you want to completely translate the extension, there is a good possibility that you will have to translate the files in that folder as well.

WHAT'S NEXT?

In this chapter, you saw how to translate complete extensions, using Joomla's file system.

In the next chapter, we'll show you how to translate single text strings, using Joomla's administrator interface.

CHAPTER 13.

TRANSLATING WITH LANGUAGE OVERRIDES

In the previous chapter, we showed how to translate an extension where there's no translation available.

However, there is a simpler solution available when you need to translate only a few language strings. This solution is easy-to-use and certainly quicker than translating all the language strings for an extension.

Joomla has a feature called "Overrides", which allows you to override existing language strings.

In this example, we'll translate the same "Read more" string from OSDownloads that we translated in the previous chapter.

- In the Joomla admin area, go to "Extensions", then "Language(s)" and finally click on "Overrides":

- On the Language Overrides page, click on the language filter, and choose "French (FR) – Site":

- Click on the "New" button:

- On the next page, search for the text string that you want to change:

Search text you want to change.

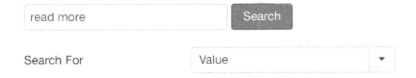

You have to use the specific language constant in order to create an over
Therefore, you can search for the constant or the value you want to chang
By selecting the desired result the correct constant will automatically be in

| read more | Search |

Search For | Value ▼

- With text as common as "Read more", there are likely to be several results. In this example, click on "COM_OSDOWNLOADS_READ_MORE":

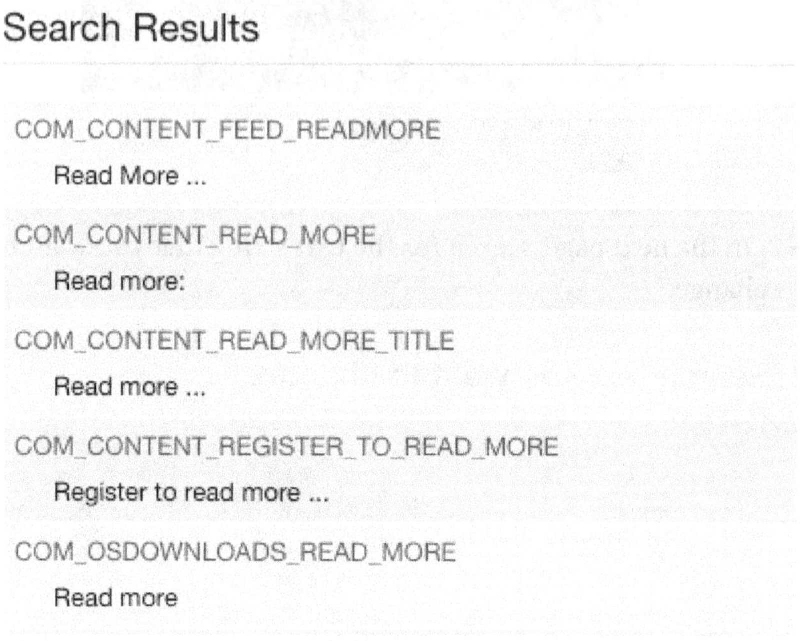

Search Results

COM_CONTENT_FEED_READMORE

    Read More ...

COM_CONTENT_READ_MORE

    Read more:

COM_CONTENT_READ_MORE_TITLE

    Read more ...

COM_CONTENT_REGISTER_TO_READ_MORE

    Register to read more ...

COM_OSDOWNLOADS_READ_MORE

    Read more

- Fill in your translation in the "Text" area:

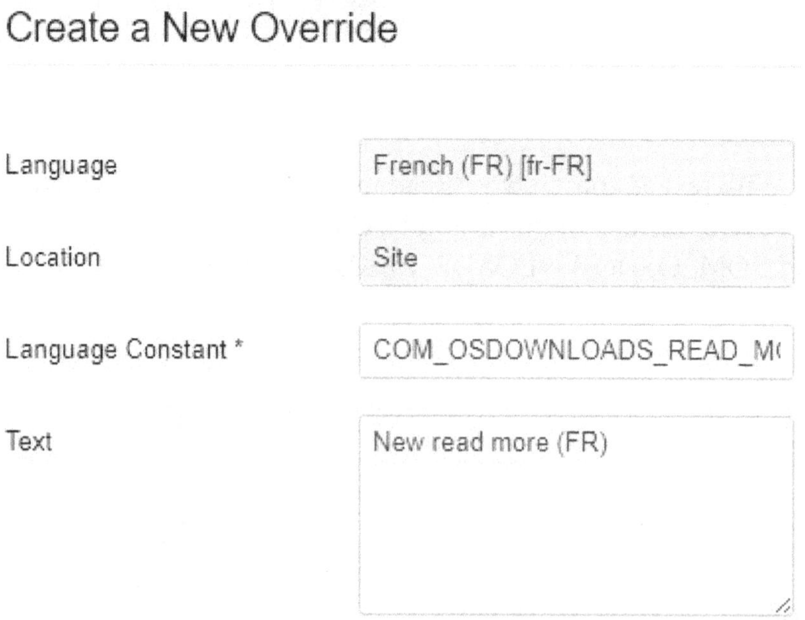

Create a New Override

Language	French (FR) [fr-FR]
Location	Site
Language Constant *	COM_OSDOWNLOADS_READ_M(
Text	New read more (FR)

- Click on "Save & Close".

- You should see the new language override in the list of available language overrides:

	Constant ▲	Text	Language Tag	Location
☐	COM_OSDOWNLOADS_READ_MORE	New read more (FR)	fr-FR	Site

- If you switch to the front end of the site and visit the French version of the download section, you will see that your new language override is working:

CHAPTER 14.

CONCLUSION

We hope you enjoyed the book and its content. Building multilingual websites is a serious business and depending on the complexity of the single language site, adding multilingual capabilities can be a tricky task.

We tried to give you an overview of all the options and capabilities built into the core of Joomla.

Joomla is advancing in its features with every new version, so it may be that some features and processes explained here will be even easier in the future. For example, we would love to see in Joomla's future versions an easy way of handling the language files for the extensions that don't have specific language translation files ready. If future versions had this, you could create new language files easier than digging into the file system of the site and manually copying, pasting and renaming the files that a specific extension is using.

We wish you all the best with your multilingual projects. Having completed this book, you have a good starting point. We hope you will find it a valuable resource of knowledge and tips on how to best approach and use the multilingual features in Joomla and your website.

If you have any questions, we're always available. Email us via books@ostraining.com.